OVERCOMING MEDIOCRITY

OVERCOMING
Mediocrity©

**A Unique Collection of Stories From Dynamic Women
Who Have Created Their Own Lives of Significance!**

Presented by Christie L. Ruffino

DPWN Publishing
www.overcomingmediocrityteam.com

This book is a compilation of stories from numerous experts who have each contributed a chapter and is designed to provide information and inspiration to our readers.

It is sold with the understanding that the publisher and the individual authors are not engaged in the rendering of psychological, legal, accounting or other professional advice. The content and views in each chapter are the sole expression and opinion of its author and not necessarily the views of DPWN Publishing.

For more information, contact:
DPWN Publishing
A division of the Dynamic Professional Women's Network, Inc.
1879 N. Neltnor Blvd. #316, West Chicago, IL 60185
www.overcomingmediocrityteam.com
www.dpwomen.com

Printed in the United States of America

ISBN: 978-1-939794-01-7

Dedication

To every woman who does not believe she makes a difference and to every woman who believes she can move a mountain.

To every woman who makes sacrifices for those she loves but doesn't make sacrifices for herself and to every woman who prioritizes those moments when she can pamper and take care of her own needs.

To every woman who believes that she should settle for the life she has, regardless of her own unhappiness and to every woman who has overcome great odds to create her own life of significance.

To the women in this book who have created their own personal lives of significance and for the women in my life who believe I am significant.

The Power of a Story

"And so my prayer is that your story will have involved some leaving and some coming home, some summer and some winter, some roses blooming out like children in a play. My hope is that your story will be about changing, about getting something beautiful born inside of you, about learning to love a woman or a man, about learning to love a child, about moving yourself around water, around mountains, around friends, about learning to love others more than we love ourselves, about learning oneness as a way of understanding God. We get one story, you and I and one story alone. God has established the elements, the setting and the climax and the resolution. It would be a crime not to venture out, wouldn't it?"

— Donald Miller

Introduction

For the past 10 years, the main focus of my life has been to create and manage a professional networking organization for women in the Chicagoland area that would not only provide them the opportunity to meet other dynamic and professional women, but to also provide them additional resources to assist them in their personal development and to offer them avenues to receive greater exposure for their business. So when I was asked to participate as a contributing author of Michelle Prince's anthology book, *Dare to Be a Difference Maker, Volume II*, it did not take me long to recognize the real value of that opportunity and birth the same opportunity for my members with this anthology book.

That was only a few short months ago and I have since launched a new resource for the members of the Dynamic Professional Women's Network, Inc., called DPWN Publishing, and also published this *Overcoming Mediocrity* book, which is a unique collection of stories from women who have created their own lives of significance. These women have not only created significance in their professional lives, but in their personal, physical and spiritual lives as well. We have some inspiring stories from established leaders who are making an impact on a larger scale as well as from those who are making a difference and impacting a select few in their everyday lives. These stories are meant to inspire and encourage women to realize their true potential.

We hope you enjoy our stories and feel inspired to share your own story someday.

I can promise you your story is just as significant!

Christie

Table of Contents

Christie Ruffino

My Blessings in Disguise

I was asked in a recent interview to share one thing about myself that most people may not know. That was easy I thought, because although this fact is a very organic part of who I am and well known to my family and close friends, most others are very surprised to hear it and are often skeptical about its validity. Due to the nature of the business I built and the various roles that I am required to perform, it seems to be a hard concept for many people to accept I am an introvert.

I did not always put myself out there in the public's eye as an expert in the networking world and as the founder of the Dynamic Professional Women's Network. I would never have even considered speaking as an authority to one or two people let alone to a room full of professionals. I liked being the wall flower and I would much prefer blending in with the crowd. I would rather have the attention focused on others rather than on myself. There were very few photos of me in my youth, because I would hide from the camera or stick my tongue out at the photographer. This would make those shots useless, but now my image is pasted on numerous websites, marketing materials and electronic marketing resources.

Being an introvert does not mean that I am now or ever was a hermit. In my case, it means that I prefer having a few close friends as opposed to being friends and chatting with everyone. It means that I was more comfortable at home reading than being the center of attention. In reality, if I would have been told 20 years ago this is where I would be now, I also would have been very skeptical it was true. I probably would have denied it vehemently. However, like every other person in the world, I had to adapt and evolve to the circumstances in my life to survive.

Earning an income to support myself was never something I even had to contemplate for the first 36 years of my life. I'm not saying that I was financially irresponsible in any way. I got my first job when I was 15 because I recognized the value of the all mighty buck and knew that if I wanted more "things" than my single mother could provide, I had to earn the money to buy them. I always sought out and landed the jobs I desired, but supporting myself was never the motivation.

At an early age, I fell in love and got married. I was instrumental in launching, developing and running my husband's business while managing the financial and marketing affairs. The burden of maintaining an adequate cash flow remained solely on my husband's shoulders. It was only after that life came to a screeching halt that I had to make some major changes in my life on many levels.

I was not only a "single woman" having to support myself, but also a single mom. I had two children to support on my own while also struggling through an ugly and unnecessary divorce battle. During this process, after surviving a period of major depression, I went on autopilot and managed one day at a time. I could not let the poisonous feelings associated with the loss of my marriage, an angry and spiteful ex-spouse and being virtually broke keep me down. That is not to say that I did not have numerous days when I felt utter despair and hopelessness, but through my new found Faith and the knowledge that my children were counting on me, I managed to continue to take it one day at a time. I created a plan to manage what little assets I had and I found employment that would help me take care of my new financial burdens.

What if the trials of our life are just blessings in disguise?

It is funny that when we are in the midst of our worlds being upside down, we can never see how anything good could possibly come from it.

However, when the dust settles and time has elapsed we can reflect and see the good that shines through. It was during this turbulent chapter of my life that I connected with some new friends who were strong in their faith and who embraced me despite my circumstances. You see at this time most of the people whom I thought were my friends did not want to hear about my problems or help me in any way. Therefore, I had to mourn the loss of their friendship as well. My family remained my rock to cling to when I started to drown. My new Christian family helped to guide, support and teach me how to believe and trust in God. They also connected me to my new job in the mortgage industry and it was this new direction that led me down the road to where I am now as the Founder and President of the Dynamic Professional Women's Network, Inc. and a John C. Maxwell Certified Strategic Business Development and Prosperity Coach.

I was hired by a great company in my area that not only originated loans, but also funded them. This company gave me the opportunity to build a strong business because I had a large variety of products at competitive rates. I provided my customers with the best experience possible in the closing process because the funds were always there on time. This was during the height of the mortgage refinance boom and the competition was fierce. Leads were not provided. I had to find new business on my own or I would not get paid. I had always been a natural networker by sharing the great resources I had established with my family and friends. However, it was never an intentional strategy. I had to become a more proactive networker by becoming a great resource myself to meet new people and gain business.

I joined a few local Chambers of Commerce but I was just one of the many mortgage professionals attending their events. My results were minimal and slow. I knew that I was on the right track, but I needed to make more progress and make it faster. It was at this time that I was invited to attend my first referral group meeting. What a great idea, I thought, since my product was of such a personal nature it made sense for me to become involved with an industry exclusive group that focused on building relationships with other professionals who would refer me business as one of their trusted referral partners. It was perfect!

The only problem now was that since the industry was so saturated with loan officers, I was not able to find a local group with my business category open. Now what? Well, through a series of events and introductions, I became part of a brand new independent group that allowed me to selectively invite other women to join based on the business they represented and the level of professionalism they dedicated to manage their business. I could assemble my own trusted referral team.

Now the DPWN story begins...

That initial group only lasted a few months. The organizer of that group stepped down and since I had already become committed to our little network, I decided to continue with the plan under our own name which became the DuPage Professional Women's Network. I researched the policies of the other well-known referral groups in the industry and came up with what I thought was the best of them all to form the initial foundation of that group. Our biggest variation from the other national referral organizations is that we wanted our group to be female exclusive because it created a unique dynamic that differed from the other co-ed groups. It was not a matter of a women's group being better in any way, but the camaraderie and energy that women can develop together can be quite powerful. We wanted to be structured and productive but I knew that some of their policies could be improved to be more conducive to our target member, the working mom. Knowing how hard it is for moms to attend early morning meetings, we chose to hold our meetings during the lunch hour. We next looked at how the other groups met every month and recognized that since we were building strong relationships with each other, we didn't need to be sitting in front of each other every week in order to care about and generate business for each other. We therefore chose a schedule where we met twice a month on a consistent monthly schedule. Over time, we defined and refined more policies, structures and benefits of membership to make our organization stronger and a more relevant resource for professional women.

We have embraced the go-give philosophy based on the best-selling book The Go-Giver, by Bob Burg. Adopting this mindset as an organization helps in two ways. The first benefit is that it results in a more productive network, because although we track the referral generation of our chapters, we do not have quotas nor do we focus on the low producers. We instead focus on giving and serving our other sister chapter members which will result in higher productivity because we truly care about and invest in each other. If a member joins with a self-serving focus, she will not get the support and results that she is looking for unless her attitude changes quickly. Second, since our members all have this giving mentality, they will be attracted to and invite other go-givers to join their network thus making our community of go-givers larger and stronger.

What eventually developed in that initial chapter was that it became very productive and successful. We eventually had to create a waiting list of women who wanted to join, but were unable to because either their business category was already occupied, or the chapter had reached its capacity. It was a great problem to have after working so hard to accomplish success, but I began feeling guilty for turning away so many women. Then during one of our leadership planning meetings, one of the members suggested that we launch a second chapter a few towns away that she would run it because it would be closer to her business.

That was the beginning of our expansion that resulted in launching additional chapters throughout the Chicagoland suburbs, into the city of Chicago and even into Wisconsin. Since we had expanded beyond the boundaries of DuPage County we replaced the "DuPage" in our name to "Dynamic" to position us correctly with what we had become. I even had to eventually make the decision to leave my full-time job with a steady and dependable salary to manage and grow the organization.

What started out to be an effort to support the business I was in at the time, resulted in a thriving organization that has provided me numerous opportunities to meet and help other women looking to grow their businesses in our network. Unlike the rest of my life, it was not planned and mapped out ahead of time. It has strictly been a "God thing" as I know that my life post-divorce has been guided by my Father and Creator every step of the way. I have been blessed to work one-on-one with some of the women in my organization to help them with their marketing and business building strategies and I have been placed in an environment to develop and refine my communication and leadership skills. In addition, many doors have been opened for me to meet some amazing and talented people in the industry whom have made a big impact in my life.

That is not to say there have not been a few growing pains along the way. It is a very difficult task to manage such a resource and maintain relevancy in an ever changing economy. What worked very well at one time as an opportunity for our members to connect, just does not work anymore. We have had to become more virtually oriented with our resources and remain on top of technology with our website, webinars and social media. However, it is safe to say that the Dynamic Professional Women's Network, Inc., has become a living entity of women who not only partner together to do business together, but they trust, mentor, support and lead each other to success. It is very rewarding to visit each of my chapters and see how they are achieving powerful results all on their own by following the plan created with that first initial chapter in Carol Stream only a few years ago.

So Here We are Now

My objective with this organization has been to provide our members ongoing opportunities to connect with other professionals through relationship networking in chapters, through our website resource or at one of our live events in addition to providing them multiple opportunities for professional development. We most recently introduced our members to the book writing arena through a reputable resource in the industry Michelle Prince from Prince Performance Group. With Michelle's guidance, we launched our first anthology book in an effort to provide our members the opportunity to share their stories and inspire others while simultaneously positioning themselves as experts in their industries, which will result in additional credibility and increased revenue. This book, Overcoming Mediocrity, is a unique collection of stories from women who have created their own lives of significance, not only in their professional lives, but in their personal, physical or spiritual lives as well. We have some inspiring stories from established leaders who are making an impact on a larger scale as well as from those who are making a difference and impacting a select few in their everyday lives. These stories are meant to inspire and encourage women to realize their true potential and my hope is that this book will be the first of many in a series of books with the same purpose.

What's next?

My goal for DPWN is to take this results orientated system and share it with more women far beyond the boundaries already established. Professional women everywhere can take our structure and our tools and adapt them to their geographical needs and launch their own DPWN referral community with our support. We have the on-line member and leadership support, training and resources to ensure their success. If you are interested in launching a DPWN Chapter in your area, please feel free to visit our website for more details. www.dpwomen.com

In addition, since the growth of DPWN has taken me out of the role as a networker, I feel like I have lost connection with my members which needs to change. Over the past year, I have completed an in-depth coaching and leadership training program with the John C. Maxwell team which I plan to use to begin working again with women who want to achieve greater results in their business as a strategic business development and prosperity coach.

This is the story of my past, present and future as a professional woman trying to make a difference in the world. At times, I feel unsure if it is wise to keep dedicating so much of my life trying to maintain and keep building this resource larger because of the various challenges I have faced along the way. Then each time I have these moments, days or hours of doubt, I am faced with a situation that helps me regain my clarity and faith. I once again realize that this is not my plan, but God's plan for me and I need to be honored to have such an opportunity and to be obedient to His will.

Blessings to you.
Christie

Christie Ruffino

Christie Ruffino is the President and Founder of the Dynamic Professional Women's Network, Inc., which is an industry exclusive networking organization designed to help women create partnerships with each other to generate ideas, alliances, and revenues within a structured referral generating format.

Five years since its conception, more than 1200 members have joined DPWN in Illinois and Wisconsin, recognizing it as a driving force behind the success and profitability for many of its members' businesses. This accomplishment along with other philanthropic efforts inspired a nomination and following honor as one of the most Influential Women in Business of 2009 by the Business Ledger and the National Association of Women Business Owners (NAWBO) and in 2010 with an Entrepreneurial Excellence Award by the Business Ledger.

Christie is now looking to expand her impact by working more closely with her members and other business professionals who want to build more business, provide more value and manifest a more prosperous life as a strategic business development and prosperity coach.

Christie L. Ruffino
info@christieruffino.com
www.christieruffino.com

Dynamic Professional Women's Network, Inc.
1879 N. Neltnor Blvd. #316
West Chicago, IL 60185
630-336-3773
info@dpwomen.com
www.dpwomen.com

Michelle Prince

Know Where You're Going

This morning, as I was having some quiet time, I found an old affirmation card tucked into my Bible. I hadn't seen it in a long time. In fact, I wrote it in 2004 when I was working in Corporate America, depressed and overwhelmed.

I wanted to get out of the rut that I had created for myself but I didn't know how. It was then that I decided to write down affirmations of what I really wanted for my life. This included the dreams that I kept hidden inside for too long. There was the desire to be all that I was created to be and the belief that I could one day be a difference maker in the lives of other people.

This one particular affirmation was something that I repeated for many years. I would stand in front of my mirror and say enthusiastically out loud, "I have made a decision today that I'm not going to live an average, mediocre life anymore!"

Gratefully, I sit here 9 years later, living the life of my dreams, following my passion and making a difference in the lives of thousands of people. All of this is because I affirmed what I really wanted in life. How appropriate that on this day; the day I planned to write this chapter for "Overcoming Mediocrity", that I stumbled upon my old affirmation.

What about you? What are you affirming for your life? What goals have you set? What dreams do you want to make happen? It's hard to reach success in any area if you don't have a goal in mind. People who actually accomplish their goals have a plan. It's pretty simple. They know where they're going.

It's easy to procrastinate when you're not really sure where you're going. You can wander around aimlessly for years. But if you know where you're going, you create a natural sense of urgency. You want to get there as soon as possible and experience the happiness and fulfillment that you deserve when you achieve that goal.

My passion was ignited and my dreams were clearly in focus at the tender age of 18 when I met my mentor, Zig Ziglar. At that time, I completely embraced personal development and goal setting techniques, which helped me to land my BIG goal of working for Mr. Ziglar in 1994. It was at that time that I made a commitment to become a motivational speaker and make a difference in the lives of others.

So there I was at age twenty-three, having reached a huge goal of working for Zig Ziglar. My dream came true, and every day of the three years I worked there, I was living my dream.

I can't tell you how amazing it was to know that I was making a difference in people's lives. Whether they bought a book, attended a seminar, or scheduled Zig to speak to their corporation, I knew that the content of the material would change their lives for the better. It was an incredible experience.

So what did I do at age twenty-three? I left.

It seems like a crazy idea, but the dotcom boom had just started, and I was lured away to the technology world to do software sales. For the first time in my life, I had to make a decision between two things: follow my passion or make more money.

The two options kept turning over and over in my mind. Follow my passion. Make more money. Follow my passion. Make more money. What do you think I chose? Yeah, I chose to make more money. And I did.

I quit the Zig Ziglar Corporation, and although it was the hardest decision of my life at the time, it's what needed to happen for me to be where I am today.

I spent the next twelve years in Corporate America. On the outside looking in, I appeared to be very successful. I had a great job. I was doing very well financially. I hit every one of my sales goals. On the outside, I looked extremely successful and happy.

But that was so far from the truth. I can tell you that the further you stray from your passion and purpose in life, the further you step away from true happiness. I woke up, got my kids to daycare, went to work, paid the bills...I went through all the motions, but I was not in the least bit fulfilled. I was busy being busy, but I had no purpose behind my actions.

I started asking myself questions. Is this really all there is? Is this really my life? Is this it? And when I honestly answered those questions, I began to realize that success is not a number. It is not a dollar sign or an expensive car. It is about being fulfilled and living a life full of passion and purpose. It was at that time I started repeating my affirmation, "I have made a decision today that I'm not going to live an average, mediocre life anymore!" but I still didn't really know how to get there.

I eventually came to six very tough questions that I needed to answer in order to make a significant change in my life. I will share those questions with you now and encourage you to spend some time searching your soul and answering them for yourself. They will help you find your true purpose in life, as they helped me.

Question #1:

What activities do you enjoy?

_____

_____

_____

_____

This looks like a very simple question, but let me be a little more specific. This is not what do you love to do for work, or what do you love to do on the weekends. What do you really, really enjoy? When you are engaged in this activity, time flies by. Are you with your kids? Are you teaching? Maybe you are listening to someone who inspires you. Are you leading a group? Cooking? Creating? What activity captivates you so completely that you lose track of everything else around you?

By the way, don't try to think of only one answer to this question. Write down everything that comes to mind. You can sift through your answers later and look for patterns or activities that stand out.

Question #2:

What would you do if you could not fail?

_____

_____

_____

_____

I had a really hard time answering this question when I was deep in Corporate America. I was no longer sure anymore what my purpose in life was, so I found it hard to think outside of the box that way. Spend some time with this question and let yourself dream big.

Let's take it one step further. If you could do anything in the world, money was no object (all of your bills were covered, your investments were handled, and you had no money worries), AND you had all the time in the world—and you couldn't fail—what would you do? It's interesting to ponder that question when the usual roadblocks are removed.

Would you be doing what you're doing today? Would you start a charity? Would you travel the world? Would you write a book? Write down anything that comes to mind.

I believe that your purpose in life is very closely tied to the things you enjoy, so this is not a frivolous exercise. Your answers are important to finding your purpose.

Question #3:

What ideas are you most inspired by?

_____

_____

_____

_____

There are a million possible answers to this question. You can be inspired in countless ways. Are you inspired by politics? Community concerns? The elderly?

If you're not sure where to start in answering this question, I'll give you another question: When you go to the bookstore, what section do you gravitate toward?

For me, it's always the personal development section. It makes perfect sense. That's my passion.

Where do you wander to when you walk into a bookstore? It might be the history section, or the cooking area. You can learn a lot about yourself by paying attention to where you end up in the bookstore.

Question #4:

When do you feel empowered?

_____

_____

_____

_____

What I mean by *empowered* is when you feel like you're at your absolute best. Another related question that might get you closer to your answer is: What are you doing when people compliment you? What do others think you're good at doing?

Maybe you are a terrific manager, or an inspiring public speaker. You might be a good listener or an excellent teacher. When do you feel empowered? When are you at your best? Write down everything that comes to mind.

Question #5:

What is on your bucket list?

_____

_____

_____

_____

I'm sure you know all about the movie *The Bucket List*. It's about two old guys who are about to "kick the bucket," and they make a list of all the things they want to do before they die.

Do you have a bucket list?

If you don't, sit down right now and make one.

What do you keep saying you'll do someday? Put it on the list! Someday will get here sooner than you think.

There are absolutely no rules for this list. Write down anything that comes to mind—anything you want to do before you "kick the bucket."

Question #6:

What legacy do you want to leave?

_____

_____

_____

_____

At the end of our lives, every single one of us is going to leave some kind of legacy. It's not just a legacy for your children. You will leave a legacy in your community, in your workplace, wherever you go. Your actions impact others. What sort of trail do you want to leave?

I love this last question, because it really allows you to go back to your purpose in life. What is your legacy going to be? What do you want people to remember about you? Your accomplishments? Your character? If you think about the legacy you want to leave behind, you can work backward to discover what you need to do today to develop that legacy.

If you want to leave a lasting legacy, you can't wait until the last minute. Procrastination is not an option. What are you doing today to leave a legacy? Don't put it off. This is too important to leave to someday.

These six questions are so important. Once you know what you're passionate about and what your purpose is, then you can set goals and really figure out what you want to do with your life, who you want to be, and what you want to have.

Then, begin to affirm those dreams in your mind. Really grasp the idea of those dreams coming to pass. Create your new reality. The only way this can be done, and the only way to truly be happy in life is that first you have to *know where you're going.*

Michelle Prince

As a best-selling author, Zig Ziglar Motivational Speaker, business owner of multiple companies, wife of 15 years and mother of two young boys, Michelle Prince had to learn the art of juggling her personal and professional life successfully. Most people are juggling too many things, procrastinating and not getting as much done as they want, which leads to a life of frustration and unfulfilled goals. Michelle is passionate about helping people live with purpose, follow their passion and take action in big ways! She is a self-publishing expert and teaches people how to take what they already know and put it in a format to attract more clients.

Michelle Prince
Prince Performance Group
6841 Virginia Pkwy Ste 103-124
McKinney, TX 75071
972-529-9743
Info@PrincePerformance.com
http://www.MichellePrince.com

Maureen Beal

The Leadership Journey - Not Always What You Expect

I represent the third generation of my family to lead National Van Lines, Inc. located in Broadview, Illinois. The company was started by my grandfather in 1929, handed down to my father in 1942 and then taken over by me in 1993 with my father's passing. So, now it's my responsibility to provide the hands-on family management – caring personally about our employees, associates and customers.

I've been asked about leadership on a few occasions, and the one thing that has become very clear to me is that there are many views of what leadership is – or what makes a great leader. Yet there is no one clearly defined answer on any of the leadership topics – and that's because leadership is personal. You can't read a book and become a leader. Books can make you a better leader, but leadership is the result of a personal journey. It is a journey that comes from the heart.

Now, I have to tell you that I am very proud of my company and all of my employees because they have taken our mission to heart and work very hard to maintain the customer focus that is so important in our business. In the past 15 years, National has shown significant growth along with financial stability. Our customer satisfaction levels are at their highest. I directly attribute that to our employees. They don't forget where we came from and how hard we worked to get where we are today.

They have embraced my goals and dreams for the company and continually work for improvement. How does that happen? Why do these employees feel this way? I think the answer lies in some of the lessons I've learned on my leadership journey. I'd like to share them with you.

LEADERS develop their own style

If I had to describe my leadership style today, I would have to say it's a nurturing style, bordering on motherly. And you know, for many years I was embarrassed about that because it didn't seem to fit with the leadership role models of the time.

But I smile today when I read leadership books that suggest leaders become more supportive with more team building and even more nurturing! I'm not saying that I am ahead of my time. But, as I mentioned before, I strongly believe that leadership is, in fact, a very personal journey.

I think that we should practice a version of the Golden Rule – we should treat our employees the same way we would want our children to be treated by their employers. Or, better yet, as some of your parents should have been treated by their employers years ago.

Sometimes to become better, LEADERS have to leave!

One of my success stories starts when I left the family business! I was working for National Van Lines in Los Angeles. When National consolidated its branch offices to Chicago in the 1970's, my family and I chose to remain in L.A. For the next ten years, I worked in the manufacturing industry in customer service and inside sales. Looking back, it was the best thing I could have done.

In addition to advancing on my own two feet, I was privy to conversations I never would have been invited into if I were the boss's daughter. I'd say some of my best leadership learning happened in the cafeteria, when colleagues would tell stories over lunch about their bad bosses. I learned a lot about what NOT to do as a boss from just listening.

From that cafeteria setting, I saw huge communication gaps between management and employees. So, one of the first things I did after being named National's CEO was to initiate regular employee meetings. I had seen so often how the rumor mill would run rampant through an organization when just a little pro-active communication – straight from the CEO – could have prevented that and improved employee morale.

LEADERS lead by example

Everyone says this, but it is so important. Leaders can't expect their employees to adhere to business hours if the leadership of the company wander in late each morning or leave early. They need role models, and if they think you don't take something seriously, they won't either. We can't expect employees to follow a rule that management doesn't. This is a classic case of Don't Do as I Do, Do as I Say. So I strive to be the first one in each morning – my direct reports have picked up that habit – and their direct reports do the same – it's very contagious!

Set a high standard – make sure you lead the way – and your people will follow.

LEADERS need to listen and act compassionately

These are difficult times for families and businesses in America. I am well aware of the types of pressures that this is putting on everyone. Employees need to feel valued – they need to feel that you care for them on a personal level.

As leaders we have to know when to push hard and when to ease up and give people time to catch their breath. We also need to notice when someone is having a hard time and take the time to find out what's going on. We need to be more sensitive which I believe will make us better leaders. And that takes a combination of listening and compassion.

Over the years, National Van Lines has gained a reputation as a company that not only listens to its employees, but also to the drivers who represent us. Household Goods drivers are a special mix – they have to be good at truck driving, but they also have to be furniture specialists and customer service experts. These drivers need to feel a sense of belonging, and they need someone to listen to them. They can't be a number and they deserve to be "a name." We take that very seriously. As a result, when other van lines were growing by merging companies, we sat back and listened. And one by one, high quality drivers from larger, less personal organizations started coming over to National. They were high-quality, top performers. They, in turn, brought their friends. Today our fleet is second to none, and it all came about as a result of listening and really getting to know our drivers.

The same is true of our employees – we make a concerted effort to know the employees and their families. Other organizations have made some necessary budget cuts, and I understand that, but when they eliminate family events, like company picnics and Christmas parties, I really disagree. Those social occasions, where you can get to know your employees better, and see their families grow up are priceless, and they help you to retain your most valuable resource.

Speaking of resources, this reminds me of one of my favorite employees – LeRoy Krueger. LeRoy is what we Chicagoans might call a three-peat – let me explain. LeRoy came to us as a bookkeeper when he was in his 30's and worked until age 65 when he retired. The retirement life style just didn't work for him – he was bored. So he came back and worked another 5 years. He retired the second time to spend more time with his wife and travel. Sadly, his beloved wife passed away just 6 months later. After that LeRoy was very lonely and wanted to come back on a part-time basis. By this time, LeRoy was 78 years old and he had a slightly bad habit of falling asleep in his chair in the afternoon. Employees began to worry that he would slip out of the chair and get hurt. So we did what any compassionate company would do – we bought him a new chair, with arms! I still chuckle every time I remember passing LeRoy, sitting proudly in his new chair – waving at me, and saying "Thanks, Maureen, for my new chair." He never knew the real reason we bought him that chair!

A little while later, I was faced with a new dilemma. LeRoy was still driving himself to the office. At his age, about 80 years old, his driving was also starting to suffer – and so were our large, round, concrete planters in the parking lot. LeRoy had knocked them over so many times while trying to make a nasty right turn that the neighboring company's forklift driver just automatically drove across the road and picked up the rolling planter – time and time again. We were worried about what might happen after LeRoy left the lot. I was just mulling around in my mind who I could ask to give him a ride to work each day, when LeRoy announced his retirement for the 3rd time.

But that wasn't the last of LeRoy. LeRoy began to send birthday cards to all of us – from existing employees to new employees he had never met. Why? Because we were his family, and that's just what you do when you are family! That's loyalty, and that's the culture at National Van Lines. We still miss LeRoy, but we know he's watching out for us. And the parking lot is a little safer these days.

If you treat your people with dignity and respect, they will treat customers in the same fashion. One example that really touched my heart came in a letter from the daughter of a customer.

The customer was an elderly gentleman who was suffering from dementia. He was moving to a nursing home because he was no longer able to live alone. He was upset and disoriented by the moving process. But he loved trucks.

When the driver pulled up to start loading his belongings, the gentleman was fascinated by the truck. Sensing the situation, the driver asked him, "Would you like to take a ride in the truck?" The man quickly agreed. And the driver, slowly, gently, drove this man once around the block.

It was a small kindness. It didn't take a lot of time. But it was a huge gesture.

And it helped calm and assure this man as he watched his worldly possessions being loaded on to that truck. I could absolutely feel his daughter's gratitude as I read her thank you note. And I was so proud of our driver.

LEADERS bring their values to work

Along with a strong work ethic, my mother and father had a very strict sense of right and wrong. That was passed along to my brothers and me. I bring my value system into this company, by giving back to the people who are in need or who have helped you, or your loved ones, in your time of need. I am rewarded each day as I see how my employees share my family beliefs. We actively participate in our community by getting involved with charities such as The American Cancer Society and Aspire. They work very hard to raise money for these causes. Not only does it help the charity we are working for but I truly believe it brings us all together for a common cause.

I've always known that our employees enjoy good food. For birthdays and special events, they bring in some of the very best home-made treats – but I never knew how competitive they were until we started doing fundraising for the American Cancer Society's Relay for Life. What started out as a series of bake sales escalated to full-blown breakfasts and four course lunches. We just couldn't stop – and our waistlines expanded! We were so dedicated to cooking, and spending money for a good cause, that it didn't surprise me one morning when the husband of our dispatcher, Wilma, showed up with a plate of sausages for his wife's team breakfast. You see Wilma had gone into labor while she was heating them up early that morning, and she wouldn't let him take her to the hospital without stopping by the office, first! Now, that's teamwork!

CONCLUSION

To sum this up – to take your own leadership journey – you have to have a clear sense of who you are, so that you can develop your own style and learn from life's lessons. That sense enables you to lead by example, and demonstrates your vision to your employees.

When you take the time to listen you solve problems before they blend into the background; and you see yourself and your organization through the eyes of your customers and associates. That keeps you focused on them.

When you bring your values to work and add compassion, you build loyalty and a sense of community. That creates teamwork. And that team understands how important it is to take care of customers. The end result is customer satisfaction.

Last – don't be afraid of failure, or to go through learning experiences. Those are valuable lessons. They don't make you weak – they make you human. Your employees appreciate that and respect you more when you make corrections.

I am often asked where I see myself in the future, and I have concluded that I am one of those extremely lucky people who get up each morning and celebrate going to work. When I was a teenager, I remember my father telling someone that he couldn't wait to get to work in the morning. I couldn't imagine anyone feeling that way about work! And yet today, I feel the same way. I love my job and I love the people I work with.

And I wish the same for all of you.

Maureen Beal

Since taking over as CEO in 1993, Maureen Beal has seen the organization, started by her grandfather, enjoy steady growth. She plays a vital, hands-on role; maintaining that the company should "never be so large as to lose sight of the personal connection we have with our family of agents and drivers, and of course, our customers." While National Van Lines has recently become an employee-owned company, Maureen remains at the helm and continues to support woman-owned and diversity initiatives.

Maureen serves on the Board of Directors of the American Moving and Storage Association. Having served as Chairman of The American Cancer Society Board of DuPage County, IL, she is an advocate for women's health issues. Actively involved in community service, Maureen is the past Chairman of the Board of Aspire, an organization that works with children and adults with developmental disabilities. Currently, Maureen is a Trustee for Benedictine University, Board President of the Executives Breakfast Club of Oak Brook and Board Chairman of Marianjoy Rehabilitation Hospital.

Recognized for her expertise in employee retention and sound business practices; Maureen regularly speaks at industry conventions and is frequently invited to share her approach to management as a conference speaker/panelist.

Maureen Beal
National Van Lines, Inc.
2800 W. Roosevelt Road
Broadview, IL 60155
708-450-2900
ceo@nationalvanlines.com
www.nationalvanlines.com

Lillian D. Bjorseth

From There to Here, Inner Motivation Works Everywhere

How big was your hometown? About 100,000? 50,000?

How about 20,000? 10,000? 1,000?

Maybe 500? 100?

If you haven't said "yes" yet, you have company. I grew up on a farm on the outskirts of Uniontown, MO, a town of 83 people that in many ways remains unchanged many decades later.

Why is this important to my story? Because my heredity and environment prove you don't have to attend the best of schools or be raised by parents with advanced degrees to be successful. The latter might make it easier though!

My goal for taking you on this journey is not to engender sympathy, rather to have you learn and grow from my experiences without having to experience them. I also want to empower and inspire you to jump start your career or to move forward much more quickly on your personal and career enhancement path … and to smile and laugh as you learn. Your inner motivation will determine your success.

"There"

My father had to quit school in the third grade because he was the oldest son of a large farm family. When we discussed the stock market at dinner, it was the four-legged kind.

My mother had to quit school after eighth grade ... because she was a girl! She soon fell into the role of cook and caretaker for her six siblings, father and grandparents when her mother died of blood poisoning at a young age.

My three older sisters only went to eighth grade ... because they were girls! My father didn't think girls needed any more education to be able to cook and raise a family.

One of my early happenstances is that I was born seven years after my next oldest sister, and by the time I finished eighth grade, Missouri required you to stay in school until you were 16. Dad decided my junior year when I turned 16 that since I liked school and he didn't need farm help, I could finish high school. Little did he know that I would have moved heaven and earth to finish! I had enough determination and will power for two.

I was like an only child since my sisters left home to get jobs at 16. I used my imagination to entertain myself. There were no other children within miles. I "made" my paper dolls from discarded Sears and Montgomery Ward catalogs. (Still have those paper dolls!)

Each family had a home and occupation other than farming, and my favorites had huge wardrobes down to shoes, hats and purses. The clothes had to be proportionate to the dolls, and if they faced right all the clothes had to face right ... and the colors had to match. I was astonished when my friends would put too small or too large clothing on their dolls or clothing that faced one direction when the doll's face and feet went the opposite direction! This must have been the roots for my "What We Say Before We Speak" program that covers the impressions we make through appearance and behavior.

As a child, I had no role models for what I wanted to do when I grew up. I simply dreamed of it being exciting and not involving a farm. Maybe I'd be a movie star since I read about them in the fan magazines I bought at the five and dime in Perryville, a "big" town to me since it had 6,000 people. My family was aghast at that idea and was sure I'd be much happier as a parochial school teacher. My out there was that I couldn't carry a tune, and teachers had to be able to sing ... at least all of mine could.

I didn't know that attending a one-room school that included eight grades might have scholastic disadvantages. What I did know is that I got to be with other kids all day long (yeah!), and that frequently I was the first one with my hand up ... until I was told I couldn't answer questions addressed to higher grades. I could take their tests so long as I didn't share my scores. Hey, I had to improvise since my teacher tired of calling on me during my class time even when I vigorously waved my arm.

What really boosted my confidence was when we took the Iowa Basics skills test, and the teacher told my parents that I scored several grades ahead of my current one based on national averages. I mused that must even mean St. Louis, one of the few "big" cities I "knew" since it was 90 miles away, and I had been there a few times.

Christmas programs made me realize that I had special memorization abilities, and I was upset when I didn't get the largest part. I would memorize it anyway in case someone got sick (under study?). I could present so loudly without a mike that everyone in church could hear me. And it didn't make me nervous. It wasn't until much later that I learned about the number one fear in the world: speaking in front of others ... and how people needed training to overcome it, and I could get paid to help them.

It was in high school that my love of writing and my better-than-average talent came into play. I once woke up in the middle of the night wrote a paper and went back to sleep. I thought anyone could do that at the spur of the moment. My sophomore English teacher provided the spark that helped launch my communication career. She gave us an ad-writing assignment. Mine caught her eye. I still remember the opening verse:

* * * * * *

"There's a story going round about the best detergent in town. It's a fact that we can't hide. No detergent will ever beat Tide."

* * * * * *

She wanted to send it to the manufacturer. Don't think that ever happened. However, continuing good responses from others teachers, especially regarding written and oral communication skills assured me I was "college material." An exciting career now seemed a definite possibility!

On to Mizzou

My parents thought only about the expense. I had been taught the Lord provides, and I assured them He would continue. And He did. My class ranking and no out-of-state tuition steered me to the best journalism school in the world at the University of Missouri. It still amuses me that my high school counselor tried to convince me to go to an Illinois school (with out-of-state tuition and a less highly rated school of journalism) because he had graduated from there. Scholarships, loans, summer employment and jobs throughout my four years of college made it possible.

I loved being with more than 20,000 students from my first moment on campus! My freshman chemistry class was a confidence builder. It began with my being coached in chemistry lab experiments (I never knew high schools had labs until I got to Mizzou) by someone who had attended a highly ranked St. Louis high school. By the end of the semester, I was coaching him for lab work and tests … and he appreciated it! When I got into journalism school my junior year, I loved it … and worked long hours since it was standard to put in four hours of work weekly for every hour of credit. Good preparation for entrepreneurship!

My sorority (I hadn't heard of one before I got to Mizzou) helped me polish social skills, which served me well personally and in my career. One of my early post-college jobs was to rewrite my sorority's social skills guide.

What amazed me most throughout my four years (some kids took five because they couldn't make up their minds!) was the lethargy exhibited by some of my classmates and sorority sisters. I came to realize they weren't paying most of their own way … and they were often there because someone else thought it was where they belonged. It was not their way "out."

"Here"

Fast forward to Chicago: my 6,000,000 "here" from my 83 "there."

After illuminating corporate experiences at Nicor Gas and AT&T (Bell Labs [Lucent predecessor], AT&T Computer Systems and other divisions that frequently changed names back then), I started my own speaking, training and coaching business: Duoforce Enterprises, Inc. in 1990.

Over the years, I established myself as a communication and networking skills authority. The Chicago Tribune calls me a "networking expert," and the Association Forum dubs me the "business networking authority." My mission is to help you build a new kind of wealth – social capital – by improving your face-to-face networking and communication skills.

Learning Points

I learned much from my humble beginnings on through my "here" experiences, and I am still learning! It is my pleasure to summarize the most poignant. Take those that "fit" for where you are now. Come back for those that may "fit" better in the future.

- **Accept responsibility.** Don't blame your heredity, environment, spouse or partner, friends or children. None of them is at fault. You are the sole person in charge of your success ... or lack thereof. Others may throw you curve balls. Duck or catch them; don't let them hit you.
- **Build social capital.** Start early – in elementary and high school and especially in college. (My University of Missouri bachelor of journalism degree has led to countless media interviews from other Mizzou grads who have found my online bio.) If you are already in the workforce, start building relationships today or rev up your efforts. Social capital is your network of knob turners, those people who open doors for you and for whom you can open doors. It's who you know not what you know that gets you in the door.

Teach your children, nieces, nephews, grandkids and neighborhood kids how to do it. It's one of the most helpful gifts you will ever give.

- **Understand how business is conducted.** People do business with people they know and trust or people referred to them by someone they know and trust. It helps if you like each other; however, trust and knowledge are most important. Work daily on becoming better known and trusted.

- **Experience the corporate world firsthand.** Before you can be a successful entrepreneur, coach or consultant, you need to experience the environment in which you profess to be capable of advising others. Learn to play politics in corner offices and the trenches before you call yourself an expert.

- **Listen and learn from those who have been there.** Be a sponge. Listen to anyone who will share pitfalls so you can avoid them. Pay attention to the positives so you can emulate and grow more quickly.

- **Be aware that women still are paid less than men.** Then do something about it! My generation created much more equality; much work remains to be done. Don't wait for your daughters and granddaughters to make it happen.

- **Only you can motivate you.** Your inner drive will make you a winner. If you aren't where you want to be, ask yourself how important it is to be there.

- **Give without expecting to get.** Just as you can't withdraw money from a bank without first depositing it, you can't expect business referrals without first giving them. Master networkers understand the law of reciprocity. The beauty is you don't have to keep track of your chips. The universe does it for you. Give and you will receive tenfold.

- **Share, share, share!** Find the forum that works for you whether it is a women's group, as a trainer, consultant or coach, a congressperson or a corporate leader. Then share what you know with your sisters; mentor them and be the role model they want to emulate.

Lillian D. Bjorseth

Lillian Bjorseth is synonymous with face-to-face networking in the Chicago area. The Chicago Tribune dubs her "a networking expert," and the Association Forum of Chicagoland calls her the "business networking authority." She's an award-winning relationship skills speaker, trainer, coach and a prolific author including Breakthrough Networking: Building Relationships That Last, now in the third edition.

Lillian also has positively affected tens of thousands of people in the communication skills arena with emphasis on impression management, presentation and behavioral skills. She was one of the first DiSC® certified trainers in the world for Inscape Publishing, Inc.

She has been honored three times by the Illinois Chapter of National Speakers Association with the Wordsmith and Nick Carter Awards and as Member of the Year. She was also named Outstanding Chicago Speaker by

Red Carpet Concierge and one of the Outstanding Women of the 21st Century.

Lillian has worked and played politics in corporate corner offices and trenches at AT&T and Nicor and maneuvered the entrepreneurial battlefield. She knows firsthand what it takes to be successful and she loves to share how to build relationships that last.

Lillian D. Bjorseth
Duoforce Enterprises, Inc.
2221 Ridgewood Rd.
Lisle, IL 60532
630-983-5308
lillianspeaks@duoforce.com
www.duoforce.com
www.lilliancommunicates.com
www.greaterchicagonetworking.com

Darla Claire Anderson

Soul Nudges

It's raining today. The sky is blanketed with clouds, their fullness spilling over in teardrops.

There are two elderly women living in different countries, seemingly with nothing in common except that they're the same age, are both very tired today and have taken to bed.

Nora - by the world's standards, is still quite beautiful, shiny silver hair neatly in place, wearing a jeweled hair comb that belonged to her mother, blue eyes that once must have sparkled and caught the eye of many. She looks a good 15 years younger than most her same age. She's wearing pretty rose-colored silk pajamas, and is comfortable lying under the soft blue bed sheet's made of fine Egyptian cotton and a fluffy goose down comforter. At her bedside table sits a cut crystal pitcher holding purified water, a glass half-filled and her favorite coral colored lipstick. Next to the glass sits a beautiful antique clock embossed with gold-leafed flowers and inlayed with ivory.

The clock is mysteriously showing the wrong time of day....

In the dark curtain drawn room is Nora's assistant, attending to her every need, as well as a nurse that comes and goes. The television is tuned in to her favorite show, the one she's been watching nearly every week for the past 40 years. She nods off ... her chest is heavy as the medication has made it impossible to stay awake.

Nora's life, for the most part, has been very comfortable, always making sure she didn't venture out of her comfort zone. She's never been one to take risks. SHE IS AFRAID.

Her mother told her time and again, while wagging her finger in the air, *"It's best to stay safe and not take risks, otherwise you'll end up embarrassing yourself, the family, get in trouble like so many other girls, or worse yet, you could end up homeless!"* .

Nora believed her mother because the one time she did take a "risk" she totally embarrassed herself and saw that everyone was laughing and talking about how stupid she was. That was the first and LAST time she volunteered to get up in front of a class to read a report, or for that matter, share any of her ideas again if she perceived it as being even remotely uncomfortable or risky. She's afraid.

Nora has grown children who lead very busy lives; her son lives and works in another country, she thinks it's somewhere in South America, but she's not 100% sure of which one. Her daughter and grandchildren live about an hour's drive away, in the big city. She hasn't seen or spoken to her daughter for almost 10 years, since the last family gathering.

Lately, Nora's been noticing how fast time seems to have slipped by....

Half way around the world is Claire. At first appearance, Claire shows her age as if she's spent most of her life outdoors. Her hands are tanned and dotted with age spots, the lines around her eyes are deep, yet they have the quality that looks as if she's smiling. Her hair is a bit out of control; a faded grey that lost its shine years ago is braided at the back of her head and falls over the front of her shoulder, the thin fine end reaching almost to her waist. When Claire talks there's a sparkle of joy and light in her bright blue eyes that seems to turn her old weathered face into that of a child.

She is lying in bed wearing her favorite nightgown, the one she's worn for several years. It is a bit frayed at the bottom, but very cozy and a gift from her beloved son. She's wrapped herself in a soft hand sewn quilt made with patches of colorful material she'd gathered from around the world. At Claire's bedside table is a cup made of tin with a carved teakwood handle that's filled with the cold water her granddaughter brought from the well in the center of the village. The water's not quite crystal clear (just a bit of sediment), but is known for its special healing properties. Her journal, one of many, along with her preferred writing tool of choice, a pencil, is within easy reach. Next to the journal sits an old black enameled clock that was given to her father when he was a boy.

The clock is mysteriously showing the wrong time of day....

In her room are Claire's children, two grandchildren, and her best friend for the past 40 years - who's been like the sister she never had. Outside the bedroom door are more friends and neighbors waiting their turn to visit their beloved Claire.

Early in Claire's life, she was afraid to take what she perceived as risks. But over the years the first quiet nudge from her soul had become hard to ignore. She knew there was something more that she should be doing, but just didn't know what it was. Besides, she was pretty comfortable with her life. There really wasn't anything wrong, other than her soul's persistent quiet nudge that she was put here to do something different. Something of significance.

The clocks of the women are showing the same time....

Nora is disturbed...she's now alone in her room and that empty feeling; the one that's been with her for so many years is now stronger than ever. She gazes around her room and wonders what her life would have been like if only she'd have been willing to get out of her comfort zone, and followed her desires. Maybe she'd have become the teacher she always wanted to be; maybe she would have had the wonderful family life she so longed for - if only she'd been willing to take the risk of getting uncomfortable.

She then says out loud, as if she is talking to someone in the empty room, *"Was my life all for nothing?"*.

After a long pause, Nora knows that her time is done. With several shallow breaths, she weakly speaks her last words.

"I know it's too late, but I wishhhh...... I'm so sorry..."

Claire motions her son to her side. Holding his hand, she tells him to let in those who are waiting to visit her. She's tired, and she knows it time for her to leave, but is beaming as if a light is shining upon her. Once the room is as full as it can be, Claire speaks to them in a soft voice.

"Thank you for accepting me into your community. You all know I was afraid, and so out of my comfort zone when I came here to teach."

"Thank you for opening your hearts to me, my heart is filled with each one of you. My life has had meaning."

"Death is the portal to my next great adventure! ..."

"LOVE be with you...."

* * *

This fictional story is about one woman, Nora Claire. The choices she made of either staying in her comfort zone and in her fear, or to follow her souls nudges. Not everyone is called to do something different than what they're doing, but for those of you who are; it might just be time to step out of your comfort zone and start living the life you've been called to.

We may not know exactly what we're being nudged to do. We have to trust that our Source will open the doors and guide us. However, doors won't be opened unless we have the courage to take the first step. It wasn't until I was in my mid-forties that the nudge of my soul started to get my attention. I was living a very comfortable life, a good life, living what I believed to be the life of my dreams.

No doubt that venturing into unknown territories by taking the steps to change your life is scary, especially when we don't know exactly where we'll end up. The biggest barrier to following our soul's nudges can be broken down to one thing. FEAR.

Fear disguises itself in many ways; the most potent is the Saboteur within that tells us untruths. Untruths we LISTEN to and BELIEVE.

The first time I recognized the voice of the Saboteur was when I was following my soul's nudge; developing a new creativity workshop. I'd been very excited about this and was getting close to completion. One of my favorite things to do when planning is to go for a jog. When getting in the "zone", I'm able to think clearly and get very creative. This particular morning I was jogging on the pathway that runs alongside the beautiful Tampa Bay. Just as I completed a particular session for the workshop in my head, a very loud voice said to me,

"Who do you think you are?"

"You can't do that!"

"You're not qualified to teach that!"

I stopped dead in my tracks and almost immediately what seemed like a 2ⁿᵈ voice, popped in and said,

"Don't we both want the same thing for Darla? We want her to be happy! Can't we work together?"

I actually thought that I may have been talking out loud to myself, and honestly I don't know if I was or not, it really didn't matter either way. What did matter was that I realized the voice telling me I couldn't do what I wanted to do was a very familiar one. It was a voice that had been sabotaging my plans and dreams for a very long time.

Many of us have to come to a point in our lives when we finally get fed up or mad before we make the choice to change. That day in Tampa Bay was the day I decided once and for all to take my life back. I spent the next several months paying close attention to the Saboteur, my Saboteur. My intuition was telling me not to ignore the 2nd voice. The one that said, *"Don't we both want the same thing for Darla?"*, my Muse. This is when the Saboteur~Muse Project™ came into being.

The voice of the Saboteur can sound like this:

Loser!	You're a failure
You're not smart enough	Don't embarrass yourself
No one likes me	Best to Play it Safe...

Any of these sound familiar? Of course they do, we've all heard them before. I've never come across anyone who hasn't had these types of self-limiting, bullying thoughts run through their head.

The voice of your Muse can sound like this:

I can do it!	Let's play
I am beautiful	People like me
Let's try it	Follow your Souls Nudge

The voice of our Muse isn't nearly as obvious as the self-limiting one. We've a tendency to focus on the negative much more than on the positive. Take news, for example, bad news gets our attention whereas hearing good news doesn't have nearly the impact and hold our attention. It is the same with our own negative thoughts (the Saboteur), it's easier to believe those thoughts over the positive ones (the Muse). When left unchecked it becomes our nature, or at the least an unconscious habit, like that of a well-worn groove in a record.

Hearing Soul Nudges can also be difficult to recognize, especially when our inner saboteur takes up more space than we should allow. Another inhibitor to hearing our souls nudge, is the stream of thoughts (negative and positive) continually going through our heads all day long, leaving no room to hear your soul nudges. To change; choose to 'Be Still' by quieting our mind, halting the dialogue running in your head. How? You can do this by meditating, placing attention on your breath, or an object like a candle: just noticing....without thinking.

There's a large, deep toned bell hanging in my studio. I'll randomly ring the bell; students stop what they're doing; place their thoughts on "hold" until the sound fades away, providing a space for their souls. When we quiet our minds, even just for a moment, it gives our spirit room to connect with its Source. Creativity and intuitive abilities are activated and increased.

After developing the Saboteur~Muse Project™, I was able to move past my fears and self-limiting beliefs. Although still uncomfortable, I made the choice to put one foot in front of the other, listen to my Muse and follow my soul's nudges. Life became lighter, happier and continues to feel like an adventure. Amazingly, people who could help me would show up, doors began to open; taking me further in the direction I was being nudged. And as if by magic, my one-year old creativity business was recognized by MORE Magazine™. They did an article about 'awakening your inner artist and retreats to spark creativity for women'. Eight businesses throughout the world were featured, and mine was one of them! I did nothing to get the attention of the MORE Magazine™ people. They were led to me – they showed up! With a customer rate base of 1.3 million, I got what I'd call, pretty awesome FREE advertising! Doors opened as I chose not to listen to my Saboteur; instead I chose to follow my soul's nudge.

My next nudge was to start a women's group. I didn't really feel that this was something I was meant to do, since I was once afraid to speak in front of groups! However, I knew in my heart that it's better to have tried than to be left wondering "if only...". It doesn't mean I'm not nervous when I'm in front of an audience. It does mean I've come to love myself (including my saboteur) enough to take perceived risks. I followed the nudge and founded the Rogue Moxies™, a networking group in my picturesque hometown of Ashland, Oregon. What's fabulous is that we've become a sisterhood community. We've gone beyond our businesses, and like sisters, we support one another in our personal lives as well. If I 'd chosen not to follow my soul's nudge to start this group, I'd have missed out on an amazing group of spirited, beautiful women in business; who have my heart. They are my sisters and I am theirs. We are here for one another.

Figuratively speaking, the transformational Saboteur~Muse Project™ saved my life. It saved me from Nora's outcome; which on the surface was comfortable, but a life of mediocrity, fear, feeling unfulfilled and unimportant. I once believed that I wasn't good enough, smart enough or pretty enough. I WAS AFRAID (just like Nora). Today, I AM good enough; I have confidence and courage. I can and do teach what I know, as I have the heart to share with those willing to walk this divine path of following our soul's nudges.

Taking steps to follow our soul nudges reminds me of walking on a soft pine needle covered pathway through the Redwood forest. We can't always see the path directly under our feet, or even 10 feet in front of us. What's perceived as huge obstacles and a path that doesn't always seem to go in the right direction can stop us. Imagine looking down at the forest path from above, like a hovering angel. We would clearly see that even though the path may be crooked and look off course, ultimately when staying true to ourselves and our desires we'll end up getting through the forest and to our destination.

I doubt that my soul is leading me to a small village in another country, like Claire. But it is leading me and I still don't know exactly where I will end up (just like the crooked path in the forest). But what I do know is that once I stepped out of my comfort zone, I was committed to living the life I was put here to live. I know in the core of my being that our Soul Nudges lead us to a life of love, abundance and fulfillment and does not lead us astray.

LOVE be with you.

Darla Claire Anderson

As a self-driven Creative, Darla shares her intuitive gifts, life experience and training, through workshops, life coaching and nurturing retreats through CommittedLiving™, an organization she founded in 2009.

Committed to a Life of Freedom, Darla began a real estate acquisition & property management company (DAPA Inc.) in 1998, ultimately leading to an appearance on the OPRAH Show. She has taught homeowners "How to Get Paid to Go on Vacation" - a way of turning negative, or no cash flow residential properties into gold mines. Other financial courses on how to be debt free includes the extremely popular "Moxie Money Workshop" geared towards women.

Connecting with others is a way of life for Darla. In 2010, she founded the Rogue Moxies™, a new open style networking community for women in southern Oregon. An organization designed to bring women together to empower their lives and businesses. Through the diversity of its many members, a strong sense of sisterhood and community is formed offering creative skill building, networking, collaborating, and friendships in this unique community.

Continuing to follow her Passion, Darla created the transformational Saboteur~Muse Project™ and the "Awaken Your Muse" workshop. This program provides tools to gain self-confidence by removing self-imposed roadblocks, creating a new way to obtain success in following through with goals and dreams. This project has evolved into a successful life-coaching program with affiliated workshops. Darla's relaxed style of experiential coaching and facilitating is one of inspiration, encouragement and fun!

By implementing her Mission, Darla assists women on the journey of re-discovering their creative soul, enabling them to embrace the freedom of being fully engaged and committed to living lives of abundance and empowerment.

- Certified NLP, Hypnosis & TLT Practitioner
- Life Coach
- Master Creativity Coach

Darla Claire Anderson
Committed Living
P.O. Box 3237
Ashland, Oregon 97520
928-607-1293
darla@committedliving.org
www.committedliving.org

Linda Meeuwenberg

Conquering Fear and Living the Dream

"If we all did the things we are capable of doing, we would literally astound ourselves". Thomas Edison

Imagine yourself standing in front of a large audience to deliver a presentation. The room is quiet as you approach the podium following your introduction. Is that really me they just introduced? While my bio sounds impressive, inside I feel like a scared child. It is often said that for many people the vision of speaking in front of a large (or small) audience invokes a fear that is greater than burning alive. This phobia has a medical term called Glossophobia. Symptoms include acute hearing, increased heart rate, increased blood pressure, dilated pupils, increased perspiration, increased oxygen intake, stiffening of the neck/upper back muscles, and dry mouth which is related to the "flight or fight" response. It is estimated that as much as 75% of the general population is afflicted by this phobia. (http://en.wikipedia.org/wiki/Glossophobia)

That was me many years ago. Now, I enjoy a profitable business giving presentations to varied groups such as women entrepreneurs, Chamber of Commerce's events, Rotary and large dental and medical audiences to name a few. My topics are varied and usually involve a motivational theme combined with some type of skill building such as Communication – Making it Work for YOU! Since communication is the foundation of almost everything we engage in, I can tailor this topic to any group - from parenting to customer service.

"Expose yourself to your deepest fear; after that, fear has no power, and the fear of freedom shrinks and vanishes. You are free". Jim Morrison

I faced tremendous fear and anxiety about public speaking and still marvel that I was able to face it and walk through the wall of fear. Even though for many years I felt like every bodily event would hit me at the same time just minutes before entering the stage, I learned that once I really was immersed in my topic, it began to flow. I usually started with a dry mouth so severe that I had to stop and sip water and/or ask the audience to get involved in an exercise while I calmed myself taking steady slow breaths. I learned to take discreet calming breaths while being introduced all the while smiling as if this moment was the greatest moment of my life. One of my graduate professors used to tell us just to "Act as if…" So I acted!

"Life is either a daring adventure or nothing". Helen Keller

It began for me as a result of frustration in my employment as a registered dental hygienist in the small Michigan farming community of Fremont – home of Gerber Baby Food. I had an unpleasant encounter with the new associate dentist in our practice and decided at that moment that I did not want to work with him anymore. In the 1970's jobs were very prevalent in my field. For some unknown reason, I woke up on my day off and drove a short distance to my alma mater. I have a tendency to make impulsive decisions. I had received a letter a few years previously seeking part time instructors there. So, off I headed to check it out with letter in hand. It turned out they were in desperate need of part time adjunct instructors for the clinic where students learned to provide dental hygiene care on patients. I was immediately hired and enrolled in a degree completion program for a BS in Allied Health Teacher Education. I transferred all the additional college coursework from another university and learned I only had to complete a few more requirements to complete my BS degree. I loved being a dental hygienist and had no aspirations to be anything but a dental hygienist.

I absolutely loved teaching from the first week. Students were so fun to work with and I realized how much I had learned in the eight years of private practice experience in various offices and settings across the state. They were so eager to let me help them and listen to my stories of working with patients in the office and how it would be for them following graduation. After one semester of working part time, I was offered more hours for the next semester. My program director called me into her office one day and asked me to apply for a recently opened full time tenure track faculty position. It would require me to prepare lectures and manage the curriculum for the senior clinical class. While I enjoyed working one on one with students and patients, the thought of standing in front of 60 dental hygiene students spurred fear and anxiety.

I asked if I could take all the clinical hours of other faculty and not lecture at all. That was not an option. Fortunately, my Director encouraged me to apply and was an amazing mentor. I landed the position and my journey began into what turned out to be nearly three decades and an acquired rank of Full Professor. Achieving that rank in academia is not an easy task for a woman. One of the requirements for moving through the ranks from Technical Instructor to Assistant Professor, Associate Professor and finally Full Professorship is being able to document that you are contributing to the body of knowledge in your field. That required research papers and presentations. When I retired I had achieved not only Full Professorship but one merit pay increase beyond; the first woman to achieve that distinction in the College of Allied Health Sciences at my university. I was awarded the distinction of Professor Emeritus by the Board of Trustees in December of 2006. I left with a severe chronic pain issue from the postural stresses of dental hygiene and leaning over students combined with a genetic predisposition and two rear end collisions with whip lash injuries. It was not the way I wanted it to end.

"Whatever the new beginning is for you right now, allow yourself to be swept away by the sweet freedom that comes with it". Mark Christian

Not only did I learn to prepare and deliver lectures to students, I began submitting papers for presentation at dental educator meetings, state and national dental associations and volunteered in my community speaking to varied groups about oral health. I even earned a First Place Award from the American Association of Dental Schools, now called ADEA, for my presentation titled: Teaching Patient Centered Counseling Skills. I worked with home health care aides teaching them about oral care of their clients and school lunch personnel about the nutrition and sugar content of foods they were feeding their children. I volunteered to speak at the local Rotary club for Children's Dental Health Month and National Dental Hygiene Month. I joined the local Rotary Club as one of only three women members. I also completed two graduate degrees following the completion of my BS degree. I graduated from two different universities with Master's degrees in Guidance and Counseling and Communication, respectively. This advanced education helped me venture into new areas outside the scope of dentistry and to apply skills to dentistry and all health care fields. I developed a curriculum for nurses in communication skills as part of my first master degree and worked in a hospital as a volunteer during my second degree studying communication of patients and their practitioners. I also immersed myself in the "Writing to Learn" project on campus and attended a teacher's writing conference one summer. As a result of attending that workshop (with all English/Language teachers), they published two of my works – a short story – Violets in the Window and an essay – Where were all the Women? in an anthology of Teachers Writing - Teachers Learning. That was amazing to me as I was a dental hygienist – not an English teacher and a very odd duck out of water with that group.

Completing these additional degrees and accomplishing so much in my field including a collection of awards was pretty astounding for this small town woman. My parents had not completed high school and no one in my family had ever ventured away to college. Dad dropped out in his senior year to serve in the military and became a decorated WWII veteran. Mom dropped out of school in her senior year to become his wife after he returned from the war on Valentine's Day. They did not "have to get married". While I was away at college, both returned to school to complete the minimum requirements to get a high school diploma. They both enjoyed the classroom and were proud of their achievements.

I attribute much of my success as a professional woman to a bad marriage. My husband was a substance abuser and an alcoholic. It took me three attempts at filing for divorce before I actually finalized it. Many of the wounds from the rejection by him for alcohol and drugs were healed by achieving. Isn't that what any good Christian girl does? My parents were proud and I was hurting. I immersed myself in therapy along with my small child and sometimes even her father would attend the sessions. I wanted so desperately for us to still remain a family of some sort for her sake.

Overcoming one's fears opens all kinds of possibilities. I was a shy girl from a small farm town in Michigan and led a very sheltered life. All my extended family of cousins lived around me and we rarely traveled anywhere except to Missouri to visit my mother's relatives on Easter break. Although I sang and played piano for our church, the thought of speaking terrified me. With the help of a great mentor, becoming an expert on my topics, and a lot of self-talk, I was able to rise above it and enjoy traveling to exciting places as I perfected my craft. I have met so many wonderful people on my travels. Many of my seminar participants follow up with an email on how much they enjoyed my presentation and how much it motivated them. They stay after the program to chat and join me on my social network sites. I have a huge following of former dental hygiene students that enrich my life daily as well.

"We gain strength, and courage, and confidence by each experience in which we really stop to look fear in the face... we must do that which we think we cannot". Eleanor Roosevelt

I never intended to be a motivational speaker, yet that is how I am often billed at varied venues. Much less did I ever dream of becoming an entrepreneur and the CEO of my own firm enjoying working from my little beach house. I really only wanted to be a homemaker and mom. It was a divorce that moved me into supplementing my income with my speaking skills and thus was born Professional Development Association, Inc. in 1989.

I have given presentations in Saudi Arabia, France, Sweden, New Zealand, Canada, Mexico and most states in the USA. I absolutely love what I do and it provides an excellent source of income after retirement from university teaching. I enjoy a few extra days on my travels for pleasure or to visit friends and often have the joy of taking my daughter with me. I am living the dream in my little beach house in Cape Canaveral where I am so blessed to be able to enjoy warm tropical breezes while I walk the beaches every morning and ride my bike as often as possible. So, face whatever fear it is and get moving to live your dream. What is your dream life? I wish you all the success in your endeavors. If this small town girl can do this, then so can you!

Remember: Every dream begins with a dreamer.

Linda Meeuwenberg

As the CEO of Professional Development Association, Inc. Linda offers dynamic seminars to motivate participants to ACTION. As a member of the Chamber of Commerce, she served on the Small Business Development Council and as member of her local Rotary Club, she served as the publicity chair.

Linda holds the rank of Professor Emeritus at Ferris State University, where she was awarded a First Place Award from the American Association of Dental Schools and inducted into Sigma Phi Alpha for her contribution to education.

Linda has served on many industry boards and is listed in the Directory of Dental Speakers and International Speakers Network. She is the 2009 recipient of the Hygiene Hero Award, finalist for the Women's

Leadership Award of Central Florida, finalist for the Humanitarian Award of Brevard County, and the recipient of the coveted 2012 Sunstar RDH Award of Distinction.

She has published numerous articles, a short story, co-authored *Stepping Stones to Success* and *3D Dentists-The Future is Now*. She serves as a columnist for Access magazine and has made several TV/radio appearances. She is currently writing her next book on Conquering Fear. She is a highly sought speaker. In her spare time she enjoys acting and modeling.

Linda Meeuwenberg
Professional Development Association, Inc.
232 Canaveral Beach Blvd
Cape Canaveral, FL 32920
231-598-1749
linda@lindapda.com
www.lindapda.com

Edie Gibson

Casual Christian No More: Overcoming Spiritual Mediocrity

Mediocrity has many faces. I was a casual Christian for many years, living a mediocre spiritual life. This is the story of my walk with God that led me to a spiritually full and abundant life! If you are a casual Christian, my prayer for you is that you too embrace your faith, step out and overcome spiritual mediocrity, and walk proudly with God!

"Do not be yoked together with unbelievers...What fellowship can light have with darkness?" **2 Corinthians 6:14 (NIV).**

Being yoked to an unbeliever was more difficult and depressing than I ever imagined. However, it was when my unbelieving, alcoholic husband met Jesus Christ and started his marathon run to consume His word and live in His likeness that my life began to truly spiral nearly out of control. He was lost and now is found. I was found but nearly lost. My life journey back to the love and understanding of our Lord Jesus Christ is what inspired me to write this chapter. Through this walk I have learned to accept myself with all my flaws and goofy quirks. I have learned to accept my husband where he is and walk with him, not away from him. I have a new appreciation for God and His power in my life. When I walk with Him, life is so much easier. It was when I walked away from Him that my life became total chaos.

Just then a light radiant cloud enveloped them, and from deep in the cloud a voice: "This is my Son, marked by my love. Listen to Him." **Mark 9:7 (NIV).**

Let's back up a few years. I was born and bred in Michigan, and raised in a conservative Christian household. I met the Holy Spirit when I was 16 and lost in a haze of booze, drugs, and wild friends. A friends' Mom suggested that I attend her church. I brushed it off, of course. I woke up that Sunday morning and was compelled to check it out. I was greeted by joy, singing and numerous hugs. I found myself in the front row, unheard of for me! The preacher asked if there was anyone that needed healing and if so, to step forward. I had my eyes closed and was humming along to the music. My friend placed her hand on my lower back and gently pushed me forward. I took a step and opened my eyes to see my friend deep in prayer and her hands raised high. She had not touched me! No earthly person had. Immediately, the preacher and the prayer team surrounded me and started to pray over me. I was a bit dumbfounded but seemed to feel a sense of calm. I was then escorted to another room where they promptly tried to get me to speak in tongues. I ran for the door!

I raced home and went straight to my room. As I lay in my bed with my eyes closed, a warm, calm sensation seemed to start at my toes and radiate up and out of my body. I opened my eyes. I was enveloped in a glow of sparkling light that was pure love! I knew at that instant that it was the Holy Spirit surrounding me. I smiled and cried. When He was about to leave, I begged Him to stay. He said He would never leave me. Then, He was gone! In that very moment, I knew God would always walk with me, that He would always love me, that He would always take care of me and that I would meet Him again! I had no idea I would not truly know Him again until I was in my late 40's!

Enter the Youngblood

They say that a girl grows up and marries a man just like her father. In hind sight, I guess I did, somewhat. Who'd of thunk he would present himself as a long haired, ski-racing, quiet, HOT, Harley riding young blood. His name is Chris.

Welders, wine and wildness filled my first visit to the Blue Lake Lodge in 1988, a beautiful serene place owned by Chris's mom and where my friends ran to heal. My life changed forever one weekend when I first saw Chris walk across the front lawn to go swimming. My heart dropped. I "knew" at that instant that he was going to be my husband. He was 20 and I was 25. He had not gone to college and I was well on my way to a successful career. A passionate summer fling kept us entangled in each other until he left for college three months later. I was heartbroken. I kept track of his life through his Mom. I was living with an emotionally unavailable, heavy drinking man and living a busy materialistic life on the east coast. Jimmy Choo, Calvin Klein and Ralph Lauren were my best friends and took all my money! What a wardrobe I created. But the wardrobe and Saab convertible were not enough to fill my soul. I found myself wondering what had happened to Edie.

"They mingled with the nations and adopted their customs: They worshiped their idols: which became a snare to them." **Psalm 106:35-36 (NIV).**

I stood on the train platform in Westport, CT one winter day heading into the World Trade Center for work. I looked at my outfit, added up the cost of my shoes, stockings, skirt, blouse, blazer, jewelry, coat and handbag then multiplied it by 50. OUCH! Who was this well dressed, callous, materialistic, spiritually empty person that had taken up residence in my body? I had lost my soul to New York City and needed to get out FAST! A few months later I fled back to Michigan to heal. Chris was also ending a relationship and life in Montana and about to flee to Michigan to heal as well. God had a plan for us but I had no idea what it was. I really had no idea that God was the one calling me to Michigan. I was so far away from my faith it never occurred to me that this was His plan! We rekindled our love and began our journey together. We moved to Crested Butte, CO in August of 2001, married in 2002, and will celebrate 11 years of marriage this May, 2013! However, our pathway to peace was steeped in pitfalls and pain. We have endured the loss of our unborn twins, financial devastation and the loss of friends as we walked towards Christ, and near destruction of our marriage. But God had a plan!

"Blessed are the poor in spirit, for theirs is the kingdom of heaven. Blessed are those that mourn, for they will be comforted" **Mathew 5:3-4 (NIV).**

My husband Chris is an unapologetic believer in Jesus Christ who is celebrating recovery from an addiction to alcohol. In January of 2006, I asked him for a divorce and kicked him out of the house because of his drinking. He promptly checked himself into a 28-day treatment facility. There he found sobriety and his peace, and God found him! During his 3rd week at *Charm School,* Chris was struggling with understanding the faith aspect of sobriety. He turned around and there He was, Jesus himself, sitting at his desk, smiling. His jumbled brain was made clear. He has not faltered one step since this meeting.

I, however, proceeded to lose my peace and my way. The Evil One was thrilled to have me in his claws and supremely mad that he had lost his grip on Chris. I was poor in spirit and mourning. I was still very angry at my husband. I did not want to be married to him but I had taken a vow before God to stay in my marriage "till death do us part." I was dead in spirit so why couldn't I leave him? Makaila, our daughter is why. She did not ask to be born and I know God brought her to us to bind us for life. I am forever grateful.

"Blessed are the meek, for they will inherit the earth. Blessed are those who hunger and thirst for righteousness, for they will be filled." **Mathew 5:5-6 (NIV).**

During the midst of all the turmoil, I decided to quietly untangle myself from my husband financially. Against all odds, I opened a private dental hygiene practice called About Face Dental Hygiene Spa. I was told it would never work, that it would never make money and that I was crazy for trying in our small, rural ski town. Once again, I overcame mediocrity and my business thrived. In 2009, spinal surgery ended my full time clinical career and I was forced to close my practice. I hit bottom. I was meek, hungry, and thirsty. The real estate market had also crashed and we lost everything. Everything materialistic, that is. Again, God had a plan!

Chris had discovered this "program" that incorporated the 12 Steps of AA with a spiritual, Christ centered focus. He discovered Celebrate Recovery (CR) and it changed our lives, his more quickly than mine but I am running to catch up! As he embraced his faith and new role leading a CR program in our church, I began to look the other way and stray from my walk with the Lord. I remember looking in the mirror one morning and did not know who was looking back at me. A Christian therapist and friend asked me what my passions were and I could not answer. I could tell you my husband's but I had no idea what made my heart sing. I had become gray instead of Technicolor. I had entered what John Baker, author and creator of CR, calls the "cycle of despair", guilt, anger, fear and depression. I was spiritually empty.

"Blessed are the merciful, for they will show mercy. Blessed are the pure in heart for they will see God." **Mathew 5:7-8 (NIV).**

I was ready to break the cycle of despair and get back to God! I was sick and tired of being sick and tired, just like an addict. I had become co-dependent with my husband and it nearly killed my spirit. I started the process of forgiveness. I began to forgive my husband and myself. I started working the "little sister" program of CR called *Life's Healing Choices*. I admitted need, sought help, let go, and started to come clean about my past. I am currently repairing my relationship with my husband and we are on the right path! FINALLY! Praise God!

"Blessed are the peacemakers, for they will be called sons of God. Blessed are those who are persecuted because of righteousness, for theirs is the kingdom of heaven." **Mather 5:9-10 (NIV).**

I am now focused on my progress not on being perfect. I am no longer a casual Christian. I am a proud, talk about it unapologetic believer! My husband warned me that the Word could divide. We have lost friendships because of our walk with God, but the new Christian relationships we have formed are everlasting! I am maintaining momentum and growing in my faith. I am sharing my story to spread the good news about our Lord. I have overcome a mediocre spiritual life and I am continuing to pursue an abundant life with God. I hope you join me on this journey!

"You are the light of the world. A city on a hill cannot be hidden." **Mathew 5:14 (NIV).**

Navigating the pathway of spiritual transition through change is never easy. Through trial and error, I found a way through and out of the turmoil created by life with an alcoholic. If this chapter resonates with you, I pray you find your peace, as I have, living with a recovering addict and in the grace of God...every day! Celebrate Recovery saved our lives! I urge you to seek out this program and dive in!

With Blessings and gratitude,

Edie

Edie Gibson

Edie Gibson, BSDH, MSc, is, above all, an unapologetic believer in Jesus Christ, a wife, and mother to her greatest blessing Makaila. She is a charismatic, knowledge-wealthy trainer with a mission and passion to affect CHANGE by empowering women to "put on Christ" and wear their faith with passion! She incorporates real world experiences and humor into all her programs, making difficult subjects fun, empowering, and thought provoking. She owned an independent dental hygiene practice, called About Face Dental Hygiene, in Crested Butte, CO until spinal surgery ended her clinical career.

Edie is the founder & CEO of IHS Empowerment Group offering life-changing seminars designed to empower participants to "*get unstuck from their stuckness*" and move into their peace. She is also a Clinical Trainer/Advisor for The Implant Consortium, a Corporate Trainer for

Balancing Life's Issues, Inc. and an independent speaking professional. She is a Regional Assimilation Coach for Celebrate Recovery. Edie is pursuing her MS in Psychology and training to be a Licensed Addictions Counselor. She is the Volunteer Coordinator for CASA, Voices for Children and, along with her husband Chris, runs a Christ-centered transitional living facility for men recovering from addictions called The New Adams House. Edie also served on the Editorial Review Board for the Journal of Practical Hygiene, is a Thought Leader for Hu-Friedy, a Key Opinion Leader for Crown Seating and PDT Inc. and published author.

Edie Gibson
IHS Empowerment Group
PO Box 13
Crested Butte, CO 81224
970-596-4458
Edie@EdieGibson.com
www.EdieGibson.com
www.IHSEmpowermentGroup.com

Carrie Steuer

My "Lopsided" Blueprint of Balancing Motherhood and Career.

Like many women, my story starts out the same. You have grandiose ideas of what you want to be when you grow up. Maybe you went to college. Maybe you knew exactly what you wanted to become. Maybe you stumbled upon a career. I assure you, no little girl ever stated the words…"When I grow up, I want to be 'A Bra Lady'".

My Korean immigrant parents modeled a "work to the bone" work ethic so I grew up not knowing any other way. Seasoned with scholarships, coveted internships and a fancy college degree, I was ready to conquer the world. I had my road map in place. I was going to graduate, get a great job, get married, wait a few years to have kids, put them in daycare, and be this wonder woman balancing her career and family and live happily ever after. This is where my blueprint was an EPIC FAIL and looked nothing like that cookie recipe you downloaded at Christmas and attempted from Pinterest.

I accomplished those things that I set out to do. I found joy in crossing things off my list. I graduated, got a job, waited a few years to have children and regularly vocalized to my husband that I was going to be a working mom. I imagined daycare, carpools, gymnastics, and eating on the run to soccer practice. It's what I thought I wanted. We now fast forward to the delivery room when this beautiful miracle was placed in my arms. My first thought was… "More than anything, I want to be a stay at home mom". Pass the smelling salts! My husband nearly passed out hearing those words. Not because he wanted me to go back to work, but because he wanted what he grew up with, a stay at home mom for his children. Husband - 1, Me - 0. But this round, I didn't mind losing.

I worked in corporate America for seven years and now here I am, a new mom, elbow deep in diapers, car seats, a talking dinosaur on television, and completely convinced that my baby was the cutest baby in the world. I embraced the new role of Mommy. It was a role every mother expects, but in my case, I didn't expect it to become full-time. To be clear, I have never regretted my decision to be a stay at home mom, not then and not now. Even though my husband was able to provide for our financial needs, transitioning from a two-income household to a one-income household was an indulgence that did not come without sacrifice. I knew the days of freely dining out, supporting a shopping habit and vacations were now luxuries instead of the everyday.

However, I couldn't ignore the voice in my head about my parents' sacrifice in coming to this country for the sake of their children, my education and career and the loss of my income, because up until that point my identity was so wrapped up in a career role. I missed the salary, the bonuses, company matched retirement plans, the grown-up business trips, the adult interaction and even the mundane things like getting dressed and being made-up for work.

When my second child was nearly two, my brain was begging to be exercised. I yearned for conversation that did not involve potty training or a talking train. So I put my feelers out and half-heartedly scanned the help wanted ads. I felt trapped between my desire to remain a stay at home mom and wanting to contribute financially to the family in a non-paper route, stuffing envelopes, and assembly-from-home type of job. One fateful Saturday, I attended the typical suburban arts and craft fair with a friend. It was at this particular craft fair that I came to a crossroad where I would meet what would challenge and help refine me into the person I am today. It was a road that I would not have chosen otherwise. It was the path of direct selling.

I never considered sales a career option for me, let alone direct sales selling. I felt that because I had a college degree, sales in some way was beneath me. In some distorted way, I considered it "begging" and didn't see the longevity in direct sales. Sure, your mom and your friends buy to support you, but then what? I feared being a burden and worst of all, I didn't want my family and friends to feel obligated. However, I couldn't ignore this overwhelming feeling of potential and opportunity. In fact, I didn't realize how much I enjoyed the product and how much it was on my brain until a friend of mine said, "If you like the product so much and it made that much of a difference, why don't you SELL it." This is what I mean when I said I never considered myself a sales person; it wasn't even on my radar.

A conversation I had during my last year in college with a friend who had graduated a year earlier stood out vividly in my memory. I asked him what he was doing, and when he replied he was in sales, I was stunned. I couldn't understand why someone who graduated with high honors would take a sales job. My thoughts were "Ah, poor guy, he couldn't find real job. Better luck next time". What I didn't know at the time was his one-year post grad sales job was paying him a six-figure income.

After a fierce inner battle, I allowed myself to be open to the opportunity of direct sales. In some ways, it made sense to me. I could work a night or two a week and still be available for my children during the day. My desire to reclaim my former self and identity was a constant calling that I could no longer ignore. I love my family with every fiber of my being, but I needed something to call my own. I felt as if my identity was so wrapped up in being a wife and mother that I forgot to be myself.

The little that I knew about the direct sales industry was mostly wrong. How many of us have received the dreaded home party invitation, rolled our eyes and thought, "Not another party?" Have you thought to yourself "What is the cheapest thing I can buy in this catalog?" However, I knew of friends of friends in the direct selling industry that were in it for the long haul and heard of these stories about vacation incentives and paychecks, all with a flexible lifestyle. It intrigued me, but I was still suspicious. What I didn't know was there was a sleeping giant within me that was looking for an opportunity to make a difference in my life, my family's life, and the lives of others.

The company that caught my eye specializes in professional bra and undergarment fittings to make a woman look and feel confident while offering comfort and support. You expect this sort of service and product at the mall but not at a craft fair. I was intrigued but very skeptical of their claims and was anxious to see for myself if their declarations were true. I stepped outside of the dressing room and not only had I been wearing the wrong size bra, but the transformation was extremely visible. I was an instant believer but more importantly the hamsters in my head were working double-time. I was excited by the product and service but even more so with the potential opportunity. My initial goals were just to make enough for our monthly car payment and help subsidize the extras in life, disguised by gymnastic lessons and Little League fees and perhaps somewhere down the line something as lofty as family vacation to Disney.

Every day we are all faced with opportunities. What each of us decides to do with them, however, is what makes us great or want to kick ourselves with regret for not trying. I cannot even fathom how different my life would be today had I not pursued this opportunity in direct sales. A friend advised me saying "You can always make more money, but real opportunities in life are few and far between." With that I was sold. I nervously signed up to become a representative and decided to give it a try.

My motto for my new business became **"I'd rather have a life of *oh wells* than a life of *what ifs"*.**

Early in my new career, my goals were simple. If I worked one night a week and had a handful of shows a month, it could give us a cushion in our family budget. The resulting balance of motherhood and career left me content. A few months later at a team meeting, I was reminded that the income potential in direct sales could more than replace the salary of a corporate job. Now let's pause there. This is something I had already known about and heard stories of "friends of friends" who had made it "big". Yet suddenly, this information that I had known all along seemed to have an entirely different meaning. It was at that moment that my goals were redefined; tangible and more importantly, they became real and fiercely personal.

My formula for goal setting is a simple four-step process. **Step one** - Define your goals. Unfortunately, most people never get past this step, because they don't specifically define their goals. The desire to be successful is there but how to get there is often the mystery meat that can't be explained. If you don't know what your goals are, how will you know if you've achieved them? **Step two** - Work towards it. Ask yourself, what did you do today to work towards achieving your goal? I adopted the philosophy of touching your business every day. It might be a quick phone call or email, a team meeting or taking care of a customer. Whatever it is, don't let a day go by without being in touch with your business. **Step three** – Achieve it. Through your hard work and diligence, you've achieved your goal. Give yourself a high-five and celebrate your accomplishment. Great job! **Step four** – Rinse and repeat. Rinse your slate clean and repeat the process all over again. Not only has this life lesson served me well it has allowed me to coach my team members into reaching their own goals. It is a skill set that I hope to model and teach and pass along to my own children.

I'll be the first to admit, goal setting is inspiring for about two minutes. After that, it's scary. You find yourself perfecting your procrastination skills. It's the unknown, and let's be honest, it's a whole lot of work. But let me share with you what my goal setting projects have done for me.

- By the end of my first year, I had not one but two car loans paid off.
- In my second year, I assumed the mortgage payments on our home.
- In my third year, I took my family for a week vacation to Disney World.
- The following year I earned my company's vacation incentive and took my family to Maui.
- The next year, I bought my husband a new car. The salesman said in all of his years in car sales, he has never witness a wife purchasing a car in cash for her husband. Game, set, match!
- And most recently, the home we purchased in an overinflated market on a 7/1 ARM 10 years ago we now have the ability to become mortgage free.

If you told me eight years ago, that my dabbling in direct sales would give my family the gift of financial freedom, I wouldn't have believed that it was possible. My involvement in direct sales has given me the opportunity to have my cake and eat it too. This is an industry that I never considered and even looked down upon and yet it has given me one of the greatest opportunities I could have ever asked for.

It goes without saying that the obvious benefits of a job or career are mostly financial. However, in my journey of finding the balance of motherhood and career, an unexpected gift was presented to me in the form of my own personal development. Because of this opportunity, I was able to re-invent myself within the parameters of what I wanted for my family and myself. Although the compensation can be great, it is the opportunities that are astounding and when you tally all the benefits of this business, it has far exceeded my wildest expectations. I am a businesswoman, a professional bra fitter, a public speaker, a mentor, an advocate on women's health and self-image, but most importantly, I am a working mother.

My goals have changed again. For now, my sights are set on working towards a worry-free college education fund for my children. But my story continues and the journey has just begun, so stay tuned.

To be continued.

Carrie Steuer

Carrie Steuer is a former Federal Agent with the EPA, with her environmental skills hardly at work as a stay-at-home mom, wife, professional bra fitter, author, one-time songwriter and occasional recycler. She is Essential Bodywear's first Two Star Director.

Featured as one of six "Moms who made money from Direct Sales" in Family Circle's October, 2011 issue, Carrie's career sales of $750,000+ is the company's top producer and is on track to exceed her personal sales goal of $1 million. An annual top performer in personal sales, recruiting and team building, she has expanded her horizons to include sales coaching and mentoring. As result, she manages the largest, highest producing, award winning team in the company 8 years in a row.

Carrie is passionate about women's health and making a difference in their lives in both product and opportunity. She has participated in a variety of fundraisers and has been invited as a guest speaker at various hospitals, health care events, career conferences, team meetings, training calls and image consulting. She is also ELITE Leadership Certified with the DSWA.

Carrie enjoys spending time with her family and is a music and art enthusiast. Her other hobbies include nocturnal bike riding, competitive "rock, paper, scissors" tournaments, dialing for dinner reservations and secretly dancing to techno music in her Hello Kitty pajamas.

Carrie Steuer
312-515-5819
carrie@carriesteuer.com
www.carriesteuer.com

Jacqueline Camacho-Ruiz

Being a Lifelong Learner

My friends and I were playing a game of tag in the square when the call rang out that there was a fire. My mother came to me and grabbed my hand. We walked, sometimes ran, and then walked again to the top of the hill where my home sat overlooking the small town of Malpaso, Mexico. Red orange flames danced in the windows. The heat splashed against my young face and hands, harsher than any southern sun in summer. Our brick home loomed like an oversized oven, its contents burning willfully inside.

An inventory of things trapped inside ran through my head as I tightly clutched my mom's hand. My favorite blue dress, the doll my cousin gave me, my pink bedspread and … my beloved books. When I thought of my books, I winced the hardest. At a very young age, I fell in love with reading. For me, the turning of a page was a path to places I dreamed of visiting someday—places with snow or families who lived in opulent homes or ships that sailed on the high seas. And while the books of my youth lay in a heap of ashes inside what once was my home, I steeled myself to never forget what I had learned from them. Knowledge was something no one could take away from me. From that experience, I was on the path to becoming a lifelong learner. In hindsight, it has led to nearly twenty industry honors, a successful marketing company, the publishing of two books and, most impressive, a beautiful family. It helped me survive two bouts of cancer and face my darkest fears with gratitude and positivity. Being a lifelong learner saturates every aspect of my personal and professional life, giving me safe passage to my dreams.

Reading so young allowed me to devour great literature by authors like Dale Carnegie, Napoleon Hills, Zig Ziglar, and Og Mandino. "All the success that you will achieve is in direct proportion to how many people you have helped become successful," whispered the pages authored by Mr. Ziglar. And from Mr. Carnegie I learned to "make others feel important." Rhonda Bryne taught me that "all the answers are inside of you." Napoleon Hill opened up possibilities with "whatever your mind can conceive, you can achieve."

Reading about the lives of very successful people and listening to their wisdom has given me a cast of mentors who continuously feed my drive and determination. They are people who have tried and failed and tried again, just like you and me. A day has never gone by without doing something (whether small or large) that gets me closer to my vision. The wonderful part about learning is that there is no end. Every day is an opportunity to learn, apply, assess and start again.

If I could stack up all the books that have played a role in my life, the collection would tell the story of a girl hungry for an extraordinary life. When I came to this country at the age of 14, my most treasured memento was a tattered, well-worn *How to Make Friends and Influence People* by Dale Carnegie. It remains one of my most prized possessions. From my overloaded backpack during high school as an honor student to the weighty ideas found in my oversized college books, some of my favorite memories are reading about thought leaders in history, mathematical principles that played out like puzzles on the page, and the complexities of the English language.

Next on the stack would be business books. I was 23 when I decided to turn my passion for marketing into a real company. I was driven by the thought of helping others succeed in business after having worked on promotions in the hospitality industry. Where would I start? Once again, books formed bridges across my bed, the couch and my kitchen counter as I held my newborn son Leo in one hand and a book in another. I flipped pages on how to start a corporation in Illinois and struggled to keep my eyes open to finish a chapter on pricing services. The principles of great client service kept me in rapt attention and I drew business flowcharts of my future company after reading about the elements of a good business plan.

I have kept a journal for years. Readers often make prolific writers. I never intended to write a book, but one day I discovered that I had an endless ream of notes taken from my discussions with others in business as well as my professional experiences. The thought occurred to me to return the favor of all those wonderful authors who took the time to share their knowledge. Following months of late nights and many weekends, I published *The Little Book of Business Secrets* followed by *The Fig Factor* just two years later.

All of us run so hard and so fast in our lives. Being open to learning as much as possible slows us down just a bit, but in a very positive way. And it isn't just reserved for books. I have participated in knowledge sharing meetings with colleagues that have opened up new avenues of thought and really made a difference in my career. One experience, in particular, taught me a great deal about pursuing my vision. An accomplished marketing executive herself, Chris and I committed to a weekly call where we shared our goals and our progress. Through this collaboration, I learned about the types of clients best suited for my company, what my vision really looked like, how failure is an opportunity to become stronger, and my greatest opportunities.

Not far from me sits that very well worn book by my mentor Dale Carnegie, alongside a small, rectangular, crystal award with a simple gold insert. Both tell a story about being a lifelong learner as a means to bypass mediocrity in pursuit of an extraordinary life. Many years have gone by since I first read Mr. Carnegie's words, but I realize now how they were a compass guiding me to some of my most important experiences, including having the Dale Carnegie office in Chicago as a marketing client! When I walk into their beautiful office, I am grateful for how the company's namesake has touched my life and influenced my career. What about the block of crystal? It is the highest award given by the Dale Carnegie Training. Chosen almost unanimously by thirty-five CEOs during a leadership course I attended, the Human Relations award has been one of my greatest honors. It would never have been possible if I hadn't spent a lifetime searching for answers and asking questions.

Being a lifelong learner means being awake to the possibilities, even if those possibilities seem unattainable. There have been many times that I have been unsure of what path to take or frightened about a potential outcome. Then, I take out a book by Og Mandino and read this line: "I will love the light for it shows me the way, yet I will endure the darkness because it shows me the stars."

And I think to myself, I would like to learn more about stars . . .

Jacqueline Camacho-Ruiz

Born in Mexico City, Jacqueline Camacho-Ruiz moved to the United States at age 14 where she learned English in just one year. Hungry for knowledge, Jacqueline earned her college degree and became trilingual. From a very early age Jackie devoured amazing literature. Authors like Dale Carnegie, Zig Ziglar, Napoleon Hill and other business icons influenced the launch of her award-winning JJR Marketing agency in 2006.

Jacqueline earned the Emerging Leader Award by the Chicago Assoc. of Direct Marketing, the Entrepreneurial Excellence and Influential Women in Business awards by The Business Ledger and was a finalist for Latina Entrepreneur of the Year by the Chicago Latino Network and the Highest Human Relations Award by Dale Carnegie, among others. She serves on the board of Junior Achievement- Western Region, Community Contacts and the Publicity Club of Chicago. She is the author of The Little Book of Business Secrets that was published in 2010 and The Fig Factor.

She is a regular guest on TV and radio including CBS World News, CBS Chicago, WGN-TV, ABC7 News and WGN Radio 720.

As a two-time cancer survivor, Jacqueline possesses wisdom about life well beyond her years. She lives in Illinois with her husband and business partner, Juan Pablo, and her two children Leonardo and Giulianna.

Jacqueline Camacho-Ruiz
JJR Marketing, Inc.
1722 Simms Street, Suite 108
Aurora, IL 60504
630-786-6116
jackie@jjrmarketing.com
www.jjrmarketing.com

Lynn Casey

Right? Wrong?

When I was in grammar school, my mom had a habit of dragging me off with her to take part in various activities. I would strongly protest only to give in to her higher authority. I would have to dig very deep into my recessed memory to recall most of the stupid things that I was forced to take part in. One of the few activities that were not stupid was a workshop. The parts of the workshop that I recall included: visualization, memory enhancement and self-hypnosis. To this day, I continue to implement some of what I learned in that workshop. Reflecting back, self-hypnosis was used extensively. We would "go to our level" (as we called it). This is a place of security, peace, answers and comfort that could be attained in a moment.

During my school years, my studies were not high on my priority list. Do not get me wrong. I did some studying and I passed. I was interested in doing other things and not reading books, or studying geometry or world history. I do wish that I had paid more attention. Some of that geometry would help now. Surprisingly, years after graduation, I did go back to read some of those assigned books, and to my amazement they were good.

Several times when taking tests, midterms or finals I would be in a panic because I did not have a clue as to what was being asked for on the test (I wish that I had paid more attention). Desperate times call for desperate actions. I would go to my level and summon my assistants. Using the recall techniques, I was able to retrieve the correct answers.

Using the self-hypnosis and visualization techniques that I learned carried through to my adult life and into my sports life. I was on bowling teams and several softball teams (playing and coaching) and a women's baseball team. In my mind's eye, I would view several scenarios as if they were on a loop.

One scenario was playing ball. I would make a great running dive or leap to make a catch to save the game. Other times, I would make a tremendous throw or an unbelievable slide avoiding a tag. There was always an announcer giving play-by-play, such as, "Mighty Casey steps into the batter's box. The pitch --WHACK. She does it again. Another game winning hit. It's an awesome day as always with Mighty Casey. She does what it takes to win".

In the second feature in my mind's eye I would be bowling. I would bowl a perfect game or pick up a difficult spare. It was during one of these bowling "mind movies" that I learned the importance of being aware of my surroundings. I was deep in concentration viewing the pins as I made my approach.... released the ball .... STRIKE. I then did the exuberant punch into space (just like the pros do after a strike). To my rude awakening and jolting me back to reality: OUCH! I had taken my steps towards a wall and punched the wall instead of space. Maybe I should take up playing the air guitar. Nope that is not me, sports are more my style.

I grew up being a Chicago Cubs fan. I remember that I would hurry home from school to watch the end of the game. I always wanted to hear Jack Brickhouse (the broadcaster for the Cubs) call out "HEY HEY" as the Cubs hit a home run. In the 1980's, I was playing baseball and was selected to the all-star team. To my elation, the game was announced by Jack Brickhouse, now retired. I was the starting catcher. The press box was behind home plate. The acoustics for the field were set up for the fans in the stands, not the players on the field and I was unable to hear the announcements. At one point, the score was tied and the other team had two runners on base.

One pitch came in low and way outside. I dove to my right just to stop the ball from getting away and allowing runners to advance and possibly score. At that moment, I heard Jack Brickhouse announce "and a great save by the catcher". That's the only thing I heard announced at the game. I heard Jack Brickhouse announce my great save.

In 1985, I entered the Chicago Police Academy. Entering the academy was a big day for me and my family. At that time, my dad was a sergeant and now I'm a police officer too. Family and friends would inquire if I was following in my dad's footsteps. I never thought of my career in those terms. Based on some of the stories I was told about my dad, the policeman, I knew that they were huge footsteps to fill. I did not think that I could fill his footsteps. I always knew that I wanted to make it on my own. One thing that I knew for certain was that I would not disgrace myself, family, friends or the uniform. I kept those high standards to the day that I retired.

Years before I became a police officer, the late Mayor Richard J Daley made a statement during a press conference referring to the police department as "Chicago's Finest". As a police officer, I always thought of myself as Chicago's Finest. On numerous occasions someone would make reference to me as being one of Chicago's Finest. I would promptly make the correction that I *am* Chicago's Finest, not one of the finest. Whenever I made the statement of being Chicago's Finest I would always envision myself in my dress uniform, and would have a huge proud smile.

Throughout my career, I always believed in doing my job to the best of my ability and that there was no one better for the assignment. Assignments varied over the years. I patrolled and walked some of the most dangerous streets in Chicago. Sometimes I worked alone and other times I had a partner. There were times that I was assigned to desk duties. No matter what the assignment, I was the best for the assignment. I handled it.

I could have easily been consumed by negativity being a police officer. You must deal with emotions like death, violence, confusion, and chaos and many others. There is a trend to lose friends from prior to entering the academy and replacing them with police friends. This is partially because of the hours we work, what we experience, and how we cope with everything. I was fortunate. I kept my close friends from pre-academy time and made several close friends afterwards. I do understand the difference between friends and acquaintances.

To keep some kind of balance in my life, I stayed active in sports and developed other interests. To expand my knowledge, I attended a multi-day workshop. It was here that I met Debbie. To this day Debbie is a very close friend. Because of our timely attendance we were able to take advantage of an opportunity to attend a convention in Florida. The convention was several days of mini sessions, sales tables, entertainment, and local tours. The first night we were entertained by a Las Vegas hypnotist. It was a phenomenal show. (Five plus years later I still laugh thinking about the show.) The next morning was a Take Action Now session.

As I sat listening to Marshall Sylver, it was as if he was talking to me and only me. What he said made an impact on me, so I decided to attend The Turning Point, another motivational conference. Six weeks later, Debbie and I returned to Florida for the Turning Point. Here my life made a180 degree turn. I learned how to be a better person, a better friend and a better police officer. I developed a different perspective on life. My life changed, and it truly was a turning point. I did a lot of listening, took part in the exercises, and did the visualizations. During the breaks and at night, Debbie and I would discuss the sessions and events of the day.

This is one visualization exercise that I discussed with Debbie. There is an awards celebration in my honor in a huge hall at a facility unfamiliar to me, with my family, politicians, corporate executives, police officers, celebrities, and news media. Everything is in grey scale. My arm and shoulder became sore from being shaken so much. I was told "thank you", called a hero, and had a plaque given to me for being Officer of the Year.

Debbie was very kind as she informed me that I did something wrong. I needed more information and more detail. The more information she asked for, the less information I had.

Did I really do something wrong? I know what I saw. This bothered me. Sometimes I wondered how I can correct this. Do I need to correct this?

Now, fast-forwarding a couple years, I am assigned to desk duties as I am recovering from an ankle injury, incurred on duty. I encounter an armed gunman; a short foot chase ensues, followed by an exchange of gun fire, and the apprehension of the subject. (Minutes earlier the subject had shot and killed a police officer.)

Several months later, while at roll call I received a Fed Ex special delivery package. I had to read the letter several times to be able to comprehend the enormity of the letter. I realized that there was a fast approaching deadline to be met. I compiled all of the documents and materials, and met the submission deadline. A few short weeks later I met with a film crew to produce a short documentary to be shown at the awards ceremony.

A couple months later I was flown to Washington, DC during Police Memorial Week. Upon check-in, the itinerary was revealed.

In the morning, there was a brief meeting in the White House with Secretary of Homeland Security, Janet Napolitano, Vice President Joseph Biden and President Barack Obama. It was then on to the Ford Theater for the Top Cops Award Ceremony. The master of ceremonies was John Walsh, host of TV's America's Most Wanted, and several other celebrities were presenters. Jeremy Ratchford from TV's Cold Case series presented me with my Top Cop statue. There was a reception immediately following in the grand ballroom of the Fairfax Embassy Hotel. Upon my arrival at the reception, I realized that the lights were set low with not much color, and the room was packed with people overflowing into the hallway. There was a constant line of people congratulating and thanking me, and calling me a hero as they shook my hand. Some I recognized from TV and the movies;

some were wearing police uniforms from across the United States, others were executives from corporate sponsors, and city officials. Not only am I Chicago's Finest in my dress uniform with a big proud smile, I am the nation's Top Cop.

As I reflect back Right? Wrong? Who knows? It works for me and I will continue on the same course.

Lynn Casey

Lynn is the oldest of four children. She graduated from Kennedy High School in Chicago. She resides on the southwest side of Chicago with her rescued dogs (one of them with only three legs). Lynn has proudly served the City of Chicago for over twenty five years as a police officer. During her service, Lynn received Officer of the Month, several letters of commendation, and numerous Department Honorable Mentions for her dedication and investigational skills. Her awards for Distinguished Service, Valor and Top Cop were awarded on the city, state, and national levels.

Her community service includes dedicating her time to coaching girls' softball, cookie drives with Girl Scouts, raising funds for the Illinois Patriot Education Fund, collecting food for The Wounded Warriors, and obtaining toys for Toys for Tots. Lynn not only gives her time, but also her hair. She shaved her head completely bald for St. Baldrick's in order to show solidarity with the children stricken with cancer as well as to raise donations for children's cancer research. Lynn is a member of the International Blue Knights Law Enforcement Motorcycle Club having held executive offices at the local level. Lynn is Chapter Director of the Oak Lawn Dynamic Professional Women's Network. She is very proud of her Irish ancestry and is a member and Director of the Emerald Society of Illinois.

Lynn is always optimistic, hardworking and willing to help and to teach. She is dedicated in her beliefs, honest, reliable, and shows integrity in everything that she does. She is now retired and is spending more time in the community as well as developing new interests.

Lynn Casey
773-580-6525
info@LynnCasey.com

Phyllis Benstein

Fashioning a New Life

What comes to mind when you hear the word "Mediocrity"? Do you think ordinary...or average? My life has been about overcoming mediocrity with the many role models I met along the way. I'm one of those people with a strong faith in God. I strongly believe that there are no chance encounters and that everything happens for a reason. The people and the circumstances we encounter on our journey to greatness are the culmination of our being, our doing, our dreaming and the energy we put out into the universe that couples with others that we were meant to encounter.

I had very humble beginnings. My mom, Rhoda, was my hero and my biggest influence. She was a registered nurse who worked the night shift so she could get me off to school, sleep while I was at school, have a normal day and evening, then go to work while I was sleeping. My mom was confident, educated, and funny. She loved the finer things in life even though we were a bit mediocre as a family. She taught me to be the best me that I could be and not be like everyone else. Some of the other things that she taught me were that unique is special, be myself, be genuine, and see the good in everyone.

My dad, Jack, was a mathematician and computer programmer who taught me to find my passion, no matter what I decided to do in life. He said to be the best at it and to be at the top of my game. I was always a math whiz with great training from my dad. Since he wouldn't pay for me to go to Carnegie Mellon or NYU Greenwich Village to pursue another dream to be an actress, I went to engineering school.

I loved my J.OB. for many years. If you haven't heard, J.O.B stands for journey of the broke. I have four beautiful children, Rachel, Shannon, Mike, and Mack. I worked 50 or more hours a week as an Electrical Engineer for 25 years. I worked with only a few women. Near the end of my career, which I voluntarily left and self-retired from Engineering at the ripe young age of 48, I watched many others go to work in the dark, come home in the dark, work long hours, travel and be a servant to someone else's company with many sacrifices. It was running on a circular hamster wheel with no exit strategy.

My whole career was about rising above mediocrity and the masses, achieving balance and helping other women to do the same. After 13 years into my career I had 4 beautiful kids, a negative husband and an intense job. Then I met Paula, Independent Sales Director with Mary Kay. She invited my mom and me to a makeover event where I was introduced to the wonderful world of direct sales and network marketing. Thank you Paula for all you did to support me and build my confidence, while showing me the potential of a different path to overcoming mediocrity. My Mary Kay business was a chance for me to be in a nurturing environment of other women. This was step one on my journey to overcoming mediocrity. I had a new outlook on life, a new wardrobe and make up coupled with my awaking sleeping giant within me to be all that I could be. This allowed me to enrich the lives of others and to pay it forward to help other women step out of mediocrity and be all they could be.

Fast forward 10 years and I had built a Mary Kay team, earned a free car, became a director and still had that engineering ball and chain job that held me from unleashing my true inner self, dreams, and passions. God had a different plan for me. While doing a workshop and vendor event I met Toni who was a Founding Stylist with a ground floor start up handbag company Gigi Hill that was officially seven months young when we met. I was drawn to her energy and enthusiasm for the company, the products, and the vision of the two founders Gabrielle DiSantis Cummings and Monica Hillman. I had this feeling that this startup was a dare to be great situation that I should be a part of. I decided to become one of their stylists to see where it would go but with no intention of team building. I loved my Mary Kay but this would be fun, easy, and I'd get a little more organized while adding a product for those with a passion for fashion.

A week after I joined I was headed to a women's engineering conference in California and ended up having a meeting with Gabrielle DiSantis Cummings. It was amazing and I left with a renewed plan and goals to again rise above mediocrity and go to the top of her company.

Fast-forward three and a half years. I've reinvented my life and myself. I married my best friend, soul mate and confidant Harry Benstein. I became a Founding Style Leader in Gigi Hill in about five and a half weeks. I became one of the first Directors and left my engineering job 18 months later. Since my start, I have developed an organization of over 500 Stylists spanning 30 states and I have developed 16 leaders. Every day I wake up excited, renewed, grateful and passionate to start the day doing what I love and loving what I do. My passion is to help others be all they can be, follow their hearts and dreams and rise above the everyday mediocrity.

What drove me to do this and how did I do it? I loved my J.O.B. for a long time but after a while my values and passions didn't align with my life dreams and goals. I'm one to regularly evaluate what I'm doing and where I'm going. I looked up to the successful women and men in my field. Some loved it and some didn't. I made it to a level of leadership only to find that the more you work and the better you do, the more responsibility you get, backstabbing, dishonesty, office politics, long hours, travel and increasing time away from my family, friends, and the passions inside me that make my heart sing. I then evaluated what success meant to me, where I wanted to be in 5 years and what I wanted to accomplish. I turned to my mentors and role models and took some self-discovery and self-development workshops to discover and define my next steps and desired path and outcome. Some people can wing it thru life but those with written goals and a plan have more success, and end up where they intend and not happen upon it. Courage, faith, and a strong belief in myself, my abilities and my dreams inspired me to keep moving forward and not to look back. Mediocrity to me is the same as insanity, doing the same things over and over, to get by and not ahead. I have an inborn desire to be the best me, rise above the sea of mediocrity and the masses and make a difference to my family first, then work outward to the others in my life that I come in contact with.

I took some time to discover the beauty in the world around me and the rich relationships I could enhance once I embarked on a trip out of mediocrity.

I learned many years ago that women especially have lower self-esteem and confidence. This is a by-product of the daily rat race, negative environment and trying to please everyone at the expense of their own journey from mediocrity. Once a woman develops that confidence and self-esteem, she can do anything she desires, and she starts her own path away from mediocrity.

Another part of my journey away from mediocrity was changing the people I associated with and the groups I belonged to. I chose a different crowd of enthusiastic, energetic, and passionate about what they did or stood for type of person. Being in the presence of others vibrating at a higher level, made me do the same. I joined the Dynamic Professional Women's Network (DPWN) after meeting the founder Christie Ruffino and started a chapter. This network of excellence, and interactions with dynamic women, great events and tools has changed my business since joining in 2009.Through these interactions and contacts I have become a master networker, connector and collaborator. I enjoy looking for and finding the synergies between people and their businesses and passions in life!

Last year I decided to do a personal strengths and tools analysis and then took a Rainmaker course offered by Bill Walsh's Powerteam

International. It had an amazing content, resources and a whole new channel of supercharged entrepreneurs to meet and engage with. I am very grateful to Bill for the content, connections, opportunities and visibility his group has provided. Through this network, I have teamed up with Visionaries Becca Tebon who founded F.I.T. and is an amazing gift of energy and wisdom in the health and wellness field. I will continue to collaborate with her on programs and projects for enriching women's lives. At one of the Powerteam's W.I.N. events I connected with Julie Muller, chief Chick and founder of Chick's Connect. Her amazing vision to connect women worldwide as a mastermind group of women sharing, caring, supporting, and serving others sums it all up for me and is in true harmony with my passion and continuing journey away from mediocrity.

In summary, here are my lessons learned and my top 20 list of things to do to overcome mediocrity:

1) Don't work to minimums or you'll always be just average

2) Set your personal bar of excellence high

3) Every month beat your best, even if only by a little bit

4) Work to be at the top of your game, field and company

5) Define what success is for you and make it happen

6) Have an attitude of gratitude for everything you have and get done each day

7) Count all your blessings as they each are a gift

8) Have a coach, mentor, cheerleader, and accountability partner

9) Give back to others, it will come back to you ten fold

10) Enthusiasm is your electricity of life! Light up the room or meeting you are in and illuminate others

11) Everything happens for a reason, embrace those signs and seize

your opportunities, as they can be your stepping stone to greatness

12) Believe in yourself and be a role model for others

13) Make a difference every day to others, adding great value to what you offer

14) Don't keep your experience and knowledge to yourself, share and help others make this world a better place

15) Share your dreams, goals, and plans with everyone and they will manifest before you

16) Have the courage and faith to peruse your dreams

17) Surround yourself with others with similar passions, visions, and dreams

18) Connect others and be giving without expecting anything in return

19) Never stop looking at the beauty around you

20) You are only as good as your network, weave a strong one

Phyllis Benstein

"Every day I get to do what I love," says Phyllis Benstein, a former engineer who left her six figure job to pursue her passion as an Independent Style Director for Gigi Hill bags. "I connect with women who want to be organized, stylish and successful. I enjoy providing support and inspiration to the stylists on my team as well as to my customers. I try to show them that it's possible to have it all: friends, family and entrepreneurial success."

She became her own boss relying on the GiGi Hill organization and training with experts in the direct selling industry. By reaching out to others who enjoy fun, function and fashion she has grown her team to more than 500 stylists.

"When I met the founders of Gigi Hill -- two soccer moms from Los Angeles -- I was impressed by their passion to create bags that were both beautiful and functional," adds Phyllis." Being involved with this company in its early stages has been a phenomenal experience . Phyllis leads, trains and inspires her team which is consistently in the top 5 of the company, and one of only 7 teams in the company to reach over a million in retail.

As a busy mom, Phyllis enjoys being part of a business that gives her the flexibility to spend time with her family.

Phyllis is a great connector. She continuously explores new ways to help people succeed by supporting their personal and business goals. Phyllis serves in leadership positions as a chapter director of DPWN, and a 1st Vice President on the board of the Palatine Township Senior Center. She is embarking on a journey as an author and speaker to make a difference to others and help them too transition out of corporate America.

Phyllis Benstein

Gigi Hill

P.O. Box 671

Palatine, IL 60078

847-910-6039

Phyllis@buildyourbusinesswithstyle.com

www.gigihillbags.com/purseonalitybyphyllis

Simin Frazer

My Big Vision

I left Iran (Middle East) at the end of the 1970's on a "Student Visa." I did not speak much English at the time, but knew that I would get better by going to college. My plans were to graduate from college/university and then go back to Iran. However, my journey took a different turn. I followed the path I needed to follow at the time and focused on what I needed to do along the way.

I came from a strong family background. I was well taken care of and really didn't have much to worry about as a young teenager. I went to school and did what many teenagers in the Middle East do during vacation breaks, which is to just hang around with family and siblings. I was not prepared for where my life was going to take me in this amazing country, the United States of America.

I enrolled in one of the city colleges in Chicago and started my college life. My father was sending money every month in order for me to study and finish college.

After a few months, I met my ex-husband and we married. My son was born a year and a half later.

A year after my son was born; I had a tragedy in my family. My father was killed in the Iran/Iraq war at age 49. I could not attend the funeral services, due to the fact that I was not getting along with my then husband, and was not sure what would happen with my son. In addition, I clearly didn't have the financial resources to make travel arrangements. It was really difficult to live a life filled with ups and downs, and in fear.

I was about 19 when my marriage roller coaster ups and downs began. I was really young, but I knew that I could not continue. Therefore, I decided to end the marriage, which was not so uneventful! Going back to Iran was not an option, since in my country the father was given the custody to raise the child. That was not going to work for me. There was no more financial support from my family. I was on my own, with my little 3 year old at the time of my divorce. My ex-husband told me I would be forced to give up the custody to him.

I was young, terrified, confused, lonely, broke and inexperienced, but the thought of giving up my son was not one of the options I was going to accept.

I decided to make my college a part-time thing, so that I could focus on making money for survival. I gained employment at a bridal salon and a restaurant. I was barely making it, but I was living in a tiny apartment which we called home, and were stable for one year. Then the owner of the salon turned out to be abusive, so I was forced to leave.

Our lives became very difficult. I will never forget that we had to move six times within one year, in order to be safe! Even though I had no time to think, with no money or food to eat at times, I had freedom of mind and watched my son grow! I was happy, even though there were many uncertainties in my present and future. I had made many great friends for whom I am very grateful! I was fortunate to keep my son and kept looking for better and better opportunities.

Finally in 1984, I found a corporate job through one of the many great friends I had made, and began breathing a little easier. I worked nine to five every day, and had the weekends off to spend with my son. Wow! Even though, I didn't think my journey would end there, I was content for the time being. I will never forget, as soon as I got my first paycheck, I ran to the supermarket where the shopping took more than five minutes to finish. Five minutes was the norm, to just buy peanut butter and Wonder bread! I felt powerful, but not content! I sensed that my journey would not end there. I still had unfinished business for my life.

A year into my corporate job, I met my current husband and five years later we were married! Even though I had a great husband, and my life had gotten easier, I still wanted to do more and be more, not only for myself, but for other women with similar situations. I wanted to contribute to society and make a difference.

I was always getting more education along the way. In addition, I was getting counseling for various reasons including overcoming my father's tragic death. I am at peace with that now.

I lived through many different careers, made great money, traveled to great destinations, had a great life, but was always looking for something more. I wanted to do something that could be fulfilling both mentally and emotionally, where I could make a difference in other women's lives, both personally and professionally. I never forgot nor will I ever forget where I came from, and who had helped me along the way. I wanted to do my part.

In 2005, I started developing severe acne, which led to scars and an unclear complexion. It was really troublesome to me. After using all sorts of skin care products, consulting dermatologists, and trying various diets, through my best friend, I was introduced to a Swiss product line, which was sold through a network marketing company called Arbonne. My skin conditions cleared up after just a couple of months of using Arbonne products. I became enthused about the products. The business philosophy was amazing! Women helping women! I thought wow! How clever. Here I am always trying to work and make someone else successful. I realized that I can be the owner of my own business, control my life and teach other women to do the same.

Every job that I have ever worked at, I thought that I should have had a leadership role. I was told by the upper management that "you are so great at what you do, why would you want to worry about doing more?" I was never really happy with that answer, but I kept on going and did a great job, regardless.

Until Arbonne came along, not much had changed. When I became part of Arbonne, not only was I promoted into management, but I also found many women, just like myself, that wanted to do the same thing. How fascinating! Not only had I found what I was meant to do, I went through the biggest personal growth of my life while learning from other leaders in Arbonne. I found out several facts about leadership:

A. leaders are not born, they are developed
B. leadership requires compassion
C. leadership creates patience
D. leadership requires commitment

To make my Arbonne business successful, I attended many networking events, as well as many trade shows. Throughout all the events, I met a woman who introduced me to an all women networking group called DPWN (Dynamic Professional Women's Network, Inc.). I was a little hesitant at first, and thought, gosh I can't join one more group! However, when I met the founder, Christie Ruffino and learned about her philosophy of "Give first" I decided "what's wrong with me?" I joined and never looked back.

I consider myself successful!

I am not rich, I am not at the highest level in my company, but I know that I can be, by seeing other successful men and women.

What is the reason behind my belief? I think that "Being successful is a mindset!"

It's a mind over matter training, which is extremely beneficial to our growth, personally and professionally!

- I dedicate my success to my parents, who taught me to believe in myself and that it's O.K. to want more out of life!
- I dedicate my success to other women who were there for me, when I was broken, and put me back together.
- Last but not least, I thank my husband for his patience.
- I would like to thank Christie Ruffino for believing in me and pushing me to tell my story about who I am and where I came from. I greatly admire her for her drive and kindness. She believes that your story is important; your story is part of who you are.

Never have fear. You are only one step away from a lifetime of success and happiness!

Simin Frazer

My name is Simin Frazer. I am an Independent Consultant, Area Manager with Arbonne International.

I was born and raised in Abadan, Iran (Middle East), where I lived until the late 1970s. I moved to the United States to further my education. I traveled directly to Chicago and made it my home, and started my life as a student, a wife, a mother and a professional!

I educate consumers of the importance of using botanically based, personal care and nutritional products. Through Arbonne, I counsel individuals on how to live beautifully through botanically based beauty, health and wellness. I love Arbonne's commitment to and respect for nature.

I went through years of education in various colleges:

1979-1981 - Wright Jr College; studied Biology.

1981-1983 - Evelyn Echoles; hotel and travel management

2000-2004 - Moraine Valley College; Physical Education

I am always searching to get more education, regardless of the outcome.

My passion in life is to serve others. I would like to leave a legacy of what you can do for others. Since I have been with Arbonne, I have discovered that it is the right fit for what I need to do with my life.

Simin Frazer
Arbonne International
740 N. Hudson
Chicago, IL 60654
312-953-0298
siminfrazermg@yahoo.com
www.siminfrazer.myarbonne.com

Doreen Petty

A Small but Valuable Life

There was a line in the movie, "You've Got Mail," where the main female character writes, "Sometimes I wonder about my life. I lead a small life - well, valuable, but small - and sometimes I wonder, do I do it because I like it, or because I haven't been brave? So much of what I see reminds me of something I read in a book, when shouldn't it be the other way around?"

Mine is a small story, possibly not in length but in scope. It is small in its normalcy; just a normal girl from Chicago who hasn't achieved great fame and fortune, and has no plans to do so. My journey past mediocrity takes me no further than the achievement of a valuable life – one that makes a difference and cements the memory of me into other people's hearts and minds. I want a life that is extraordinary solely in its impact on the lives that other people live.

If mediocrity is a state of being ordinary – then it was normal in my growing-up world. I was supposed to be just like all the other girls from the neighborhood. I was expected to finish high-school – get a job – get married – etc. It never occurred to me to wish for anything more than this type of normal. College was not even discussed in my family. In fact, that may be what this story is all about; overcoming normalcy on the way to having a valuable life. I believe that a valuable life is achievable by anyone with the motivation and the willingness to learn how to dream. It's not about fame and it's not about fortune. It is about the achievement of a life that is chosen, rather than imposed.

The first sign that I was not so ordinary was when I started growing taller than my older sister. By the time I was in 7th grade, I stood 5'10" and graduated from high-school at my current height of 6'1." I was the tallest girl in the school or very close to being so. I knew that this was an extraordinary accomplishment, though one over which I had no control. As a girl who wanted to be "normal," I was not immediately comfortable with my height growing up. Other children were always ready to remind me that I was self-conscious about my gangly, too-long limbs. I was always put last in lines, never sat in the front row for pictures, and the tallest boy was almost always still shorter than me. Dance classes in the school gym were painfully awkward!

Around age 13, I found my salvation and a sense of pride in a quote from Abraham Lincoln, who said when asked about his height, that he was "tall enough to reach the ground." That was good enough for me. I stopped looking for ways to be just like everyone else and started looking for reasons why I was, or could be, different. Even then, it wasn't about being better, just about being myself, without critique-filled comparisons to other people such as those cute, tiny, blond and buxom girls who inevitably dated the tallest boys in high-school. Okay, I may have been comparing a little. For the most part, however, I learned to embrace my differences and look down (literally) on anyone who would dare to belittle me (pun intended!).

I did not go to college immediately after high school. I worked as many jobs as possible, starting at age 15, to support myself. Looking back, I had very few typical jobs by "normal" standards. At various points in time and rarely for more than a year or two, I worked at various jobs in various locations. These jobs included McDonalds (OK, this one was typical), a technical director for a junior theater, a nanny, a housekeeper in a hospital, a properties technician in a circus (which included a stint at palm-reading), a maid, an exercise instructor at a boutique gym, a janitor for a family cleaning business, an all-around helper in a dance costume company, shipping and receiving for a men's clothing store – and oh, yeah, I joined the Marine Corps. I had all of those jobs by the time I was 24. Then, I got my career - by serendipity rather than planning.

I applied for a job with a major telecommunications company based on a chance mention of job openings, from one person to another, which eventually got to me. A few years after working there, the company morphed into various entities, until it became something of a poster child for everything that was wrong with the industry (another story entirely). During a 28 year career, I held various positions in Human Resources. I had the most fun when I was causing trouble for the status quo and coaching people to greater heights of effectiveness and satisfaction with work and life. I loved the work and loved working with some of the most dedicated and intelligent people I've ever met. I even met my husband while working there. The coaching that I did was not always part of my assigned duties, until the last several tumultuous years. By then I had already started planning for my private coaching practice. During my tenure at the company, I completed an undergraduate degree in Business (19 years after graduating high school). In preparation for my private practice, I earned a Master's degree in Psychology, finishing shortly after an early retirement and 35 years after finishing high school.

One might see this story as one of perseverance and tenacity. Alas, no, it is more a story of procrastination and self-doubt. My primary focus after high school was on never being homeless (which I was at times during the 1970's) or hungry (which was a byproduct of homelessness and poverty). In retrospect, I realize that I became a procrastinator because I always assumed that I would fail if I tried to get what I was not sure I deserved. I did not expect success, even when I started achieving it personally and professionally. It was the process of learning that made everything possible. The more that I learned, the more that I realized I could learn. I know that no matter how much I learn, the volume of what I don't know will always be greater than what I do know. However, satisfying my constant curiosity and a gnawing "need-to-know" lighted my path to a valuable life. Learning gave me knowledge and applying that knowledge gave me proof of my inherent value. Learning also comes with a bonus. I found that the more I learned, the easier it became for me to learn even more. Using applied knowledge to help other people was like icing on the cake. I was finally making a difference, one person at a time.

If being mediocre means, as Wiktionary.com states, being, "of medium quality," which is first clarified as, "ordinary, not extraordinary, not special, exceptional, or great," then one must wonder if any human being can ever truly achieve mediocrity. The human condition is not two-dimensional – there is no single scientific study that can condense the entirety of even a single person's multidimensional experiences throughout a lifetime into a statistical analysis. The whole of a person's experience involves his or her own perceptions, built over a lifetime from cognitive and emotional processes – which are expressed in the behaviors that a person chooses to use. However, the individual's perception is not a complete picture. We must add the perceptions and interactions of other people as they intersect through time with the individual – and then add how each human is influenced in thought, emotion, and behavior as a result of those interactions.

This is part of a theoretical concept of self I call a C.A.B. Map©. It is our unique mental map of the cognitive (thinking), affective (feeling), and behavioral (acting) approach to interacting with and within an environment. Understanding a C.A.B. Map© requires an exploration of personality traits, thinking styles, emotional intelligence (EQ), learning styles, personal values, perception of self and others, as well as the building blocks (nature and nurture) that influence our development through childhood and into adulthood. It's like a fingerprint. The map, if it can be illustrated in enough detail, is unique for each individual. Unlike a fingerprint, the C.A.B. Map© evolves over time, because of the dynamic nature of human interaction and learning. By our very nature, we cannot be mediocre because we cannot be ordinary and we certainly are special.

This cannot be reflected in a bell curve. When parts of the human condition are measured (e.g., studies of perception, experience, behavior, beliefs, expectations, emotions, etc.) – they are measured in isolated constructs in order to avoid confounding variables. This is necessary for scientific study and even for understanding patterns and results. However, they are small parts of the whole. We can measure grade point averages as an example. Statistically, any large enough population will line up in a bell shaped curve on a chart, with the greatest number of people represented in the middle of the curve, and therefore labeled "average." This is also true for performance scales in work environments. By defining criteria that exist for the sole purpose of measuring, the resulting numbers will chart as a bell curve. I ask, however, what is the real value of labeling some people as "average," others as "below average," and still others as "above average?"

This is a rhetorical question because I've tried to answer it for several decades as an HR practitioner and have never really satisfied myself. I did learn that labels tend to be more effective at setting limits than they are at effecting growth. Calling someone something doesn't make them that thing. This reminds me of another Abraham Lincoln story. Abe asked the question, "How many legs does a dog have if you call the tail a leg?" The answer is 4, because "calling a tail a leg doesn't make it one." You can take from that any meaning that you want. I think the lesson is that it is easy to influence people into creating labels, but common sense and a little humor helps us to navigate the little tests life throws our way.

By the way, I am still a procrastinator. In fact, I am writing this chapter on the night before it is due to the publisher. I now know that my patterns are related to behavior and my coach (every coach has a coach, by the way) tells me that I can overcome this barrier. I have helped others to overcome the same barrier. I believe, however, that keeping the behaviors we are comfortable with is sometimes as much the right decision as changing behaviors for more effective options. Procrastination and my messy desk are my two "keepers". They are the behaviors that, for a number of reasons, will keep me company as I continue living my small but valuable life. Mediocrity may have been an expectation for my life, but it was never a reality.

Doreen Petty

Doreen Petty Coaching (DPC) helps people to achieve extraordinary personal and professional success. Doreen works as a coach to partner with people for the future they choose, to improve relationships, create opportunities, enhance behavioral effectiveness, make better choices, be better decision makers, set and achieve goals, and more. Her coaching style developed through her 20 years in the Human Resources field where she helped people to achieve success in a highly competitive corporate environment. Her true passion lies in her ability to make a difference in the lives of individuals who want more – in any aspect of their lives.

Doreen has an undergraduate degree in business, a master's degree in psychology, extensive training, and continues to be a learning geek. Her professional focus is on helping people through a strategy of positive psychology and goal-centered coaching. Clients have consistently praised Doreen's insightfulness and empathy. Her ability to see things from her client's perspective while helping them learn new ways to look at their lives makes her an amazingly effective coach and accountability partner.

With a network of specialist consultants, DPC's HR Consulting division helps business owners ensure that they provide the best possible work environment. DPC helps small businesses to enhance leadership and organizational effectiveness. Doreen is also a certified Senior Professional in Human Resources (SPHR).

Doreen Petty
Doreen Petty Coaching
25W075 Lacey Ave
Naperville, IL 60563
630-995-0317
info@coachingtheboss.com
www.coachingtheboss.com
www.doreenpetty.com
www.businesschoicecoaching.com

Tiffany Hinton

Living Miracles

Imagine being told at the age of 16 that you will never have children by a small time doctor in a backwoods town in rural America. You were raised to believe the doctor and what he said to be fact. You tell yourself "you never wanted kids" over and over again. But deep down you dreamed of a family in the country and little girls with blue eyes and blond hair. You tell yourself that "you wouldn't want to raise kids in the world today", but at the young age of 16 do you really even know what you want? You were the girl who still played with her dolls, when all your friends decided that they were too old. But somehow you convince yourself that "You never want children".

My story is about facing the truth and fighting back to achieve a childhood dream. I will share with you my journey to motherhood and the emotions along the way. I have been told there is no testimony without a test.

I was raised in a Christian home and attended Baptist grade school. I originally accepted Christ as my Savior at the young age of five. As I grew up, I was constantly involved with the church. At the age of eleven, my father was incarcerated and I began to drift away from Jesus. I could not understand why God would take my father away. I continued to attend church with my grandma on Sundays, but did not participate. I went away to college and eventually moved to Chicago for employment. I quit attending church and grew even more apart from Jesus.

Years later, I went back to the doctors for advice since I was bleeding from my digestive tract. I was diagnosed with intestinal ulcers and put on steroids. At times, I would take the highest dosage of steroids allowed with no relief.

In 2007, I was rushed to the emergency room with a severe appendix attack. I had emergency surgery and the surgeon did not recognize the tissue growing and encapsulating my appendix. Therefore, the surgeon sent my appendix to pathology. It came back with a diagnosis of endometriosis. Speaking with my Mom after surgery, I learned that she also had the disease and it had caused her to have a full hysterectomy at the age of 29. This scared and worried me. I thought the doctors were right that I would never have children and my nightmare had been confirmed.

Less than a year later, I was bleeding again from my intestines and struggling with the pain. I would go to work late when the disease would rear its ugly head and my mood was truly horrible. I sought out new doctors and was told just to take birth control pills. I tried this several times. Sometimes it was worse and every time my emotions would become extreme. I had the feeling of wanting to curl up in a hole and hide. My body would ache and the simplest touch or hug from another would send pain throughout my body. As I continued to struggle with the pain, I turned back to prescription pain medicine.

In the winter of 2009, I got in a fight with my OB and left the office in tears. I proceeded to go home and cry to my husband, who told me "to get up and do something about it." That is what I needed. I needed to be told to wipe my tears and create the change myself. I did the only thing I know how to do. I researched. I used the library, Internet, and health care community who I knew. My Dad gave me the *"Purpose Driven Life"* that year for Christmas. It was no coincidence that God knew what I needed. Not only did I research the medical field and my disease, but I also started to read my Bible again. In December of that year, I made a personal decision to change my diet to gluten and dairy free. I limited my sugar intake and began a large regimen of vitamins and minerals. The more I researched the disease, the more I understood that I could treat it by nutrition. I also began to seek church and community again. My husband and I started to explore area churches. As a bi-racial family, there were several where we did not feel welcome. A friend invited us to Willow Creek. We decided to give it a try and fell in love with the atmosphere and spirit. We started attending Willow Creek in February of 2010. I would weep at every service and did not understand why. I continued to come back to the Lord and through his guidance I was brought to a doctor who is truly a miracle worker.

God found me one of 30 specialists in the US who serve on the National Board for Endometriosis. The doctor actually listened to me and ran tests. I was scheduled for laparoscopic surgery in March of 2010. During surgery the doctor called in 2 additional surgeons, since I was the second worst case he had seen in his 30 years of specialization. The disease was growing everywhere including my diaphragm, kidneys, liver, and intestines. They removed three pounds of growths and reconstructed my organs. After the surgery, I expressed my fears to my doctor about never being able to have kids. It was the first time I cried at his office. I had taken the business approach to my health and removed all of the emotions to get through everything. He asked me very patiently how old I was and then said "you are already older than your mom when she had her hysterectomy." We discussed my ongoing treatment to shrink the implants, which were unable to be excised during the surgery. We decided to take the aggressive approach and during the summer of 2010, I was put on cancer medicine for treatment. He explained they were unable to reconstruct my fallopian tubes, but there was no reason I could not carry a child and I still had 1 ½ ovaries. We prayed and sought guidance from the Lord. On Good Friday of that year I rededicated my life to Jesus Christ my Savior. Through the nutrition and fellowship, I became a brighter and more vibrant person.

In July of 2010 my husband and I decided to pursue IVF. My insurance would pay for one time. I communicated this to my doctor, who said we would start in September. I was to start acupuncture and chiropractic treatments in August. I started the hormone injections in September. My grandparents and parents visited in late September. They asked if they could pray over me and as they laid their hands on me and prayed for God's will to be done, I wept as I felt the Holy Spirit enter my body. I had no doubts as I went for the egg retrieval and transfer. We had 7 healthy embryos. We transferred 2 and froze the other 5 for siblings. I had learned that one of the reasons the disease is so virulent in my body is because I do not produce progesterone. My doctor believed that if I was able to become pregnant three times in the next three years, I would build up enough progesterone to last until menopause.

October 10th was our transfer. In November, I went to one of my weekly appointments and got to hear the heartbeat of our child for the first time. I was so happy that I was finally pregnant and sad because my husband was unable to get off work and did not get to experience it with me. As our family knew our struggle, we both wanted to reach our parents. I was able to get Mom on the phone. She was very happy. If I were able to carry this child to full term it would be the first grandchild on both sides of our families. My husband was unable to reach his father and left a message. The next morning we received one of the calls you never want. My husband's aunt called to say that his dad was in the hospital because he had a stroke. Since my husband went to be with his dad, I tried not to worry or stress for the health of our miracle child. My father in law passed away the week of Thanksgiving. I still tear up when I think that our child will never get to know her Grandpa Hinton.

In the past year I cannot even begin to count the blessings that the Lord has shown us. The surgeon, who performed my excision surgery, forgave our debt and $70,000 was wiped clean. My health has continued to improve. We were blessed with a baby girl in May 2011 and again in September of 2012.

I have experienced many miracles in my life. My two little girls are the biggest. They are a constant reminder that miracles still happen today. They may not be blue eyed but they are blond. I encourage you to take charge of your life and steer your own course. Always question the experts and do not stop seeking your dreams. Life is in your control. Choose to live a positive life and be a positive influence for others.

Tiffany Hinton

Tiffany Hinton is a Super Mom, Business Owner, Published Author, and Crafting Extraordinaire!

Tiffany started blogging in June 2010, while going through treatments for infertility. Like many others needing to talk about struggles and at the time not having a friend she wanted to share with, instead she chose a different path. She chose to blog to an online journal, sharing emotions and heart.

Tiffany has written 3 books:

1. Winter Thyme
2. Spring Thyme
3. Gluten Free Mom Certified Cookbook

Tiffany learned in 2009 that she was gluten intolerant along with being lactose intolerance. This turned her life upside down. She didn't know where to start and pre-made gluten free items were too pricey. She started to experiment and explore cooking and baking since she still wanted to eat her family favorites. With research and practice, Tiffany can now turn any recipe into gluten and dairy free, without sacrificing the taste.

Join Tiffany as she creates and shares easy to follow projects in the Bittersweet Walnut Grove Book Series and Vphonegirl Blog - inspiring YOU to be the best woman you can be!

Tiffany Hinton
Vphone Girl LLC
255 N. Buffalo Grove Rd. Ste 5288
Buffalo Grove, IL 60089
773-234-6636
info@vphonegirl.com
http://www.vphonegirl.com

Dr. Christine Cosgrove

Can't Hold a Good Woman Down

I now realize that the journey that led me here today actually began in grade school. As I look back, I was made to believe that I was mediocre and that my intelligence was mediocre. I now know that we are not born mediocre; we are led to believe we are until the right people and situations come into our lives.

I was behind in my reading skills as a 3rd grader, so every day I had to leave my classroom to get additional help. Even at that age, I knew the other kids were thinking that I wasn't as "smart" as they were. You can only imagine how embarrassing it is to have to leave because you're not good enough to be in the same class as your peers. I was so sad and cried to my parents but they were the ones who made me see that my one on one lessons were not because I was stupid but that I was special and important enough to them that they wanted me to be better. They pointed out all the things that I was good at so that I wasn't embarrassed anymore when I left the class.

Then, as a junior in high school I had trouble with geometry class. I would come home completely frustrated, so my dad was kind enough to pay for private tutoring lessons for me. I made it through but never really grasped the concepts. Before the end of junior year, we all would sit down with our math teachers to discuss our career choices and which math class would be the most appropriate for our senior year.   I didn't know exactly what career path I was going to choose, but I had an idea that I wanted to go into health care and possibly nursing. My dream hadn't really been expressed out loud at the time to my teacher but the conversation still rings loud in my ears some 24 years later....Me: "What class do you think I should take my senior year?" Teacher: "It doesn't matter because you're probably not going to college anyway". Silence came over me as I hung my head. I was crushed. She was my teacher so she had to be right. Why would I question her? Aren't all adults and authority figures smart and always right? I never told anyone of this discussion, not even my parents because I was too embarrassed. I silently struggled my way through.

One thing I knew I was good at was sports. I had played softball since the age of 8. During my junior/senior year season, I had developed a pain in my lower back with pain traveling down my left leg while pitching during a game. My dad was going to a chiropractor and suggested that I see him too. I had a few treatments and magically the pain disappeared and I was back on the mound in no time. My dad knew of my aspirations of being a nurse and knew my love for people. Upon his suggestion, he said why didn't I look into Chiropractic....I could help other athletes get better too! I liked the idea but all that kept running through my head is how the hell can I be a doctor? Nobody knew of that conversation between me and my teacher. My dad asked his Chiropractic Physician if I could come in one day and talk to him and the doctor offered to let me observe him with patients. As I walked in, he handed me a white coat and introduced me to patients as the future "Dr. Cosgrove"! That sounded great but fear still overcame me...how could I become a "DOCTOR"? !

Much to my surprise I did make it into Northern Illinois. I knew other friends of mine who were accepted there too. I kept thinking, wow, I know they're smart so how did I get in? My parents were so proud and they encouraged my new career choice of Chiropractic as well. Sadly, my dad passed away my freshmen year of college. I was crushed because he was one of my biggest supporters. I wanted to come home and it was my mom who encouraged me to finish out my year there. It's what my dad would have wanted. Well, I couldn't beat that logic. I was a daddy's girl so I was going to finish and it was his memory that was my driving force to succeed. It wasn't the easiest journey but I did it. Now that nursing wasn't my top choice anymore, I went and talked to the Chiropractic School in Lombard IL (National University of Health Sciences). They gave me high hopes to get in and I knew what I needed to do. By May 1994 I was in! Again, I was amazed to say the least. How did I get into this school? There it was, that damn conversation again from my high school math teacher playing in my head again.

Now the real classes started; anatomy, physiology, neurology and others that ended in "ology". I was in the big leagues now. I always enjoyed school and studying even though I had to work at every grade I made. More tears flowed through the trimesters thinking whether I was really cut out for this? Because National was a smaller school, the teachers were able to spend more one on one time with the students. It was there that I learned we all don't have the same learning styles. Huh? You mean I am not stupid, I just learn differently? It was pointed out to me during an anatomy test that went bad. I did great on the lab practical but when it came to the written tests they didn't always go so well. I went to my teacher's office and he took the time to sit down with me and began asking me anatomy questions. I fired off the answers like it was nothing. He said he asked me the same questions that were on the test but stated them in a different way. What? You mean I actually know this stuff?? Thank you Dr. Bakkum. Thank you for taking the time to show me that I was more than capable and that I just learned *differently*! It also helped that my sister was a teacher and showed me some tools to study based upon the way that my brain worked! This was empowering, especially after she shared with me the same struggles she had in school. I had no idea. I just assumed she was really smart!

It wasn't until I was done with chiropractic school that I realized that my profession is so negatively viewed by the public. As a Chiropractic Physician, we focus our care on finding the *cause* of the symptom while the allopathic doctors just mask the symptoms. They are two different philosophies....when I find the cause of their symptoms I use manual therapies and natural remedies to heal the body so it can run optimally while M.D.'s use drugs to cover up the symptom or just cut out a part if it's not working right. Their way never made sense to me. ? Here we go again. I am choosing to be in a profession that is looked down upon as I was looked down upon for not being "the norm". Can a girl catch a break? Now throw in the fact that I ultimately chose to be a Chiropractic Internist, meaning I have furthered my education to specialize in the diagnosis, treatment and management of acute and chronic internal disorders, known as a DABCI (Diplomate of the American Board of Chiropractic Internists). Now I am *really* looked at as different. But that's OK, because I am used to it by now and I know that being different isn't so bad after all!!

I realize now that I was brainwashed into thinking that I wasn't good enough. Unfortunately, we live in a society that is brainwashed to think that our *health* isn't our responsibility or in our control and we have to live with the cards that we are dealt. I am thankful every day that because I was on a path of *resistance* from a young age, that it has led me to where I am today. I am in a fulfilling career with so many great people around me who see the same vision that I do. It is my passion to help my patients and others see that they don't have to live with ill health. I remind them that the food companies (packaged and processed foods), the drug companies as well as their "sick" care insurance (aka health care insurance) are *businesses* and in the business to make money the sicker they are.

I have made it my mission to teach my patients that their health is *their responsibility*! I spend countless hours educating every one of them on their particular symptoms and provide them the necessary tools that will lead them to improved health and a conscious life of prevention. I will NEVER do to my patients what was done to me, thinking we *can't* do something and not just regarding their health but in every aspect of their lives. It's all connected...if our minds have negative thoughts, our physical bodies will begin to show symptoms and suffer and if our bodies are not healthy then our thoughts become negative and our bodies will never heal properly. I strive to help my patients break this vicious cycle and teach them that we're in control and that we *can* change and don't need to a victim of our circumstances! .

Yes, taking care of ourselves is a lot of work but we're worth it. I want every one of my patients to feel empowered and we can only feel empowered if we are in control! We only have one chance at this game of life so let's live it well and give our bodies a chance to be as healthy as they can be. We can't live in a bubble and be protected from every pollutant or germ but we can all make better choices of what we eat, drink and breathe on a daily basis. It's easier to stay healthy than to get healthy! We are going to pay for our health somewhere along the way, either in the beginning for good health (Chiropractic preventative maintenance, natural, unprocessed food and drinks, vitamins, etc.) or at the end of our life for costly "sick care" for our poor health. Trust me it's much more cost effective to stay healthy!

I want to give my high school math teacher a big *Thank You*! Her negativity inspired me to be who I am today, helping those around me be the best they can be!

Dr. Christine Cosgrove

Dr. Cosgrove graduated from National University of Health Sciences (formally National College of Chiropractic). She recently completed a three year post-doctoral degree to become a Board Certified Chiropractic Internist, specializing in the diagnosis, conservative treatment and management of acute and chronic internal disorders as well as musculoskeletal conditions. Having the status of a D.A.B.C.I (Diplomate of the American Board of Chiropractic Internists), will provide Dr. Cosgrove advanced training and knowledge allowing her to offer patients a comprehensive, integrative approach to their health care needs and concerns.

Patients will receive individualized treatment plans with a strong emphasis on active patient participation. Dr. Cosgrove feels that when a patient is active in his/her care they are more likely to be compliant which leads patients to shorter recovery periods and the ability to return to their activities and daily lives in a more reasonable amount of time.

Dr. Christine Cosgrove
Center for Alternative Primary Care
980 W. Lake St.
Roselle, IL 60172
630-351-4362
drcosgrove99@yahoo.com
www.alternativeprimarycare.com

Marina Collazo

Trust in God

It is amazing to look back on my life, to see where I started and how the different paths God had planned have taken me to where I am today.

I never had a chance to go to college. Instead, I started at one of the larger insurance carriers at age 18, and that was *my college*. I threw myself into learning everything about that business, and I was quickly promoted. I was the youngest member of my department and was supervisor for over 23 women all older than me. I had to quickly learn how to make them work together for the betterment of the company. Working with this many women was at times challenging but I loved every part of it! Finding the great qualities of each of them and making sure they knew it was probably the best part of it. There were many hours at home working on stuff from work and it was starting to take its toll on my family life. When I gave birth to my second daughter, I left to raise my girls. I thought this was for the best and it was for my family but not necessarily for my sanity. I needed to have interaction with adults. A family friend suggested that I come to work for him a few nights a week at the local Mexican restaurant......I totally thought he was crazy...I was a cubicle girl, what on earth did I know about waitressing! Well I did it and I fell in LOVE with the industry. Getting to know my customers and their families was so cool and I excelled at my job. One of my regulars told me that I was wasting my talents and I should be at the local fine dining restaurant. I went to apply and they weren't hiring but the owner walked up while I was speaking to the manager and told him he had to hire me. I had waited on him at the Mexican place and he loved my personality and service! I learned so much more about the industry being there and this led to me becoming the marketing and advertising director of their restaurant group. I was going through my divorce during this time period and was struggling with many things. Even though I had a management position, I was still waiting on the big parties or special requests and bartending at night. I met many business owners, one of whom would change my life yet again.

He owned some fire & flood restoration franchises and wanted me to come to work for him in sales & marketing. I thought he was crazy and actually said "Why would I choose wine over mold??" He kept trying for a few years then Hurricane Katrina hit in August of 2005. He called me in September and said that he really needed my help in Louisiana. The first assignment was New Orleans.... "Restoration 101", you could say! In the next eight weeks, my life was truly changed. All of my other jobs were not life altering: this one was. Seeing the devastation close up, tore me apart every day. Every night I cried myself to sleep wondering how GOD could let this happen. I was raised a Christian going to Sunday school and vacation bible school in the summer and two years of high school at Walther Lutheran HS. But after getting married in my early twenties, church wasn't a priority as he was Catholic and didn't really attend. I knew a lot about God and had gotten baptized as a child. But he just wasn't a part of my life. This had to change, I could feel it. The man who hired me was a strong Christian and would email me Bible verses, and at one point he mailed me a Bible. He opened my eyes to see what was really left in this devastation: the strength and fearlessness of the people! I learned from them to always find a silver lining.

I was going to need to find a silver lining in one of the hardest things I would ever go through. My four year old nephew was diagnosed with a rare form of cancer in January of 2006 and became an angel in the spring of that year. Being the oldest of the four sisters, my youngest sister who was the mom turned to me desperately during this time. I was lucky enough that my company allowed me to work remotely so that I was able to be in New Mexico with her and actually stayed at the hospital most nights. Jeremy was a ray of sunshine, my little Red Power Ranger. We will never know why these things happen, but I do know that my entire family was pulled closer to God and have continued that closer walk since. I need to tell you what he said before he left. We were at his side and my sister was crying a lot and he said "Momma why are you crying? Can't you see the angels?" God Bless you JD.

I started attending Christ Community Church in the spring of 2006 and was re-baptized in the summer. You may wonder why I felt the need to do this proclamation of my faith again. I wanted this walk to be different than the last. I can't do anything without him and I thank him for that.

After my return from New Orleans, I was the liaison for a large insurance carrier and the restoration company on the claims that came in for Hurricanes Katrina, Rita & Ike. We worked out of Zurich towers for 7 days a week 12 hours a day. It was mind blowing how many claims there were and this was only one insurance company. My job was assisting the claims managers by connecting the right franchise for the work and scheduling it. I was covering losses from Texas to Florida....it was crazy. When we finally got the claims done I was wondering what my "real" job would be since there was no more hurricane stuff to work on. I was instructed to visit insurance agents and let them know what we do and drop off some marketing materials. This was fine for a while but it seemed meaningless to the job I was doing because we were on a preferred program loss with 90% of them so we would get the work any ways. Can you see how I might get bored? So I came up with a Preferred Customer plan that in essence is free & non-binding but if I meet with you beforehand, then when something happens on a large scale and everyone needs help you will be bumped to the top of the schedule. So I marketed this to churches, hospitals and schools and commercial buildings. I was enjoying this and it was working, I got to know my customers more personally before something happened. But yet there was something tugging at me to do something else.....God wasn't done with me yet.

In the summer of 2007, I attended a women's business conference event in Dallas, my home town. I sat in at an event they called wisdom circles. A total of 3500 women fill a ballroom and you sit randomly with 7 others. Each woman gets 2 minutes to share what their business problem or issue is, then the other women give ideas and suggestions for support. They told me to start my own company.....well this was nuts! I was a single mom with no child support and nothing to fall back on. Needless to say I started my own restoration consulting company two weeks later. I used to say I jumped off the cliff, hoping that a boat would be waiting for me. But a good friend told me I jumped off the cliff and spread my wings on the way down!

I work with independent and captive insurance agents for property & casualty, residential & commercial, property managers & facilities directors and even home or business owners directly. I have hundreds of contractors that can replace or repair anything that can go wrong from storms or accidents to your land, buildings or contents. Because I don't work with just one contractor, we keep the claims and the costs down. I am free to the insurance company and the client. I get paid out of my contractors' profit as if I was an employee who made the sale and would get a commission. It is a win -win for the contractors as I am giving them a lead they never would have gotten and they only pay me when they get paid from the job.

I love my business and I know that this is where God wants me to be. However, sometimes the weight of this world and the pressure to stay afloat gives the devil prime material to go after you. And he sure did. I had the breakdown believing that I was a failure and maybe I should get a "real job" working 9-5 for someone with a secure paycheck. This happened on a Friday afternoon. Prior to that at 11am, I had a meeting with someone that could possibly introduce me to the facilities director of a non-profit that has 401 properties. After the meeting I just wasn't feeling my positive self that this could turn into work. I met a friend for lunch and he noticed right away that I wasn't my upbeat positive self. He said to "go home and do something for yourself because we need you to motivate us". I went home to read my bible and my devotions. Our Daily Bread's message was to cry out to God....and boy did I. Still having this overwhelming weight, I knew the only thing I could work on would be emails. The most recent email was from the man I met with at 11am. It was an introduction to the director and his cell and two addresses that needed work and I was to call him right away. I sucked it up and put on my positive voice and called. He asked me a little more about my business and I said how I thought God wanted me to start it so I could be an advocate for the client and keep contractors in line with their costs. He said he was there to tell me that God prompted him to reach out to me and that it was the devil bringing me down. You see he had been in the building while I was meeting with his coworker and he kept getting drawn to the office while I was in there. He had to leave so he never met me but when his coworker called him to give him my info he told him to email me right away so I could call him. He knew through the divine hands of God that he couldn't wait until the next time he was in his office next week to get my card. Our God is so mighty and only he can get us through anything we go through including disasters, divorce, death, bankruptcy & foreclosure. And he shows up at the most amazing times!

I truly believe GOD has a job for me: Running my business and letting other women know that they can do anything and that they should surround themselves with positive people. At the 2009 women's business conference, a lady came up to me and said she had been looking for me all weekend. Though she couldn't remember my name, something I had said to her the year before had changed her life. I had told her to live her life for herself and to get away from negative people. She has since increased her business five-fold and has never been happier!

"Be positively FEARLESS, sisters, and trust in the LORD that you WILL do great things!"

Marina Collazo

Marina Collazo has been helping people with different disaster issues for many years. Her insurance background enables her to work well with her clients. She spent 8 weeks in New Orleans after Hurricane Katrina seeing firsthand how to help people in a disaster. She is an advocate for the client while keeping claims and costs down! Restoration Coalition is her baby that she came up with in July of 2007. She has brought together contractors from all industries that are the best in their fields. Whether your loss is large or small, residential, commercial or institutional, she has the right people anywhere in the country for the job!

She is a single mom of two beautiful young women. She is very involved with her community and with the senior community. She sits on the board of her local Chamber of Commerce and is an Ambassador for many other groups and associations. She is a very active member of Rotary and volunteers and supports her church and multiple charitable organizations.

Marina Collazo
Restoration Coalition
40 Bosworth Dr
Glendale Heights, IL 60139
630-805-0651
marina@marina-marketing.com
www.marina-marketing.com

Ann Leslie

You Are So Loved

It was the most curious thing. I knew that I was sharing Clarence's observation of the people in the room, which included his body lying dead on the bed. Thirty feet below us in the tiny room were seven people: Ron, his mother, aunt, sister, me, the nursing home administrator and Ron's father, Clarence, on the bed.

It didn't seem strange that there was no ceiling between the two of us and the people 30 feet below, although I knew it had to be there physically. There was only profound calmness and peace.

'*Well, that's interesting.*' I thought.

My body was alive. Clarence's body was dead. And although I didn't see him next to me, I was aware of his presence while we watched everyone below. Nobody was talking.

Clarence had been dressed in a plain long sleeved plaid shirt and blue jeans. His hands were resting one on top of the other just below his waist as though he was relaxing. I had the impression that he was tired and worn out from life. But what was remarkable was the room. Similar to dense smog, the deeper I looked down into it, the darker it appeared. There was no color, no white or even black, only deeper graduations of gray even into the furthest shadows.

Remarkably, as I moved back and higher above the room, the darkness dropped away significantly and become increasingly clear, lighter and brighter. Behind me there was intense radiant light, no heat, just blinding brilliant light. I never turned around to see what was there and it never occurred to me to look.

'Is this what we really look like to everyone on the other side of life,' I wondered, *'Is this what energy, density, vibrational matter look like?'*

The best analogy to describe this effect would be to stand on the side of a lake during a sunny day peering down through the water. With the sun at your back, the further down you gaze into the water, the harder it is for the light to penetrate the depths. From your perception, it becomes gradually darker and harder to distinguish details. From the viewpoint of the fish that live in the water, the amount of light is just fine and they don't notice the difference.

Dispassionately, I wondered how I could be standing there in the room and not fall down. Neither Ron nor the women had noticed anything wrong with my body while it stood next to them near the foot of the bed.

* * *

Three hours earlier, I had received a call from my neighbor across the pond wondering if he could come over and talk.

When Ron got to my home, he was distraught and miserable. He settled on the couch with a cup of coffee and plenty of refills.

Ron looked like an elf, an oversized elf, but an elf nonetheless. Sporting a mustache and a head of hair that defied being groomed, he was about five foot eight and stood ramrod straight.

I once spoke to a retired Secret Service Agent who had been assigned to President Truman's detail. Truman would take a walk every day. He called it his daily constitutional and he would take it when and where he wanted with his security detail running around trying to make him secure. It was a vastly different time and place. We would call him a free-range President.

Ron was definitely a free-range walker. He also took a daily constitutional when and where he wanted as well. Like Truman with his erect posture, he was equally at home in either the rural or urban landscape where he would disappear. Vacations and weekends were chosen with care so that he could both walk and enjoy the details and calmness of his time alone.

Since I love traveling to new places and exploring them, I found a companion in arms with Ron. He would talk at length about his trips to places I hadn't visited. They included many national parks out West with vast exotic landscapes and views. Other trips would be closer. There were numerous park districts filled with miles of meadows, river systems, rolling hills, rich prairie and dense woods in Wisconsin, Indiana, Iowa and Illinois.

Ron's constitutional in cities he was visiting would take him into nineteenth century churches where he would covet the antique pipe organs. These were the rare, fine instruments of their day. Most of them were still well maintained. Ron would play beautiful music in the churches, if he was allowed, to the delight of priests, ministers, and lucky passersby.

Ron had a joyful spirit that would not be contained. He would always choose freedom and exploration in his life over the simple routines of work, home, work, and home.

He was most likely a reincarnated elf or an escapee from the North Pole.

Ron had been the second to the youngest of five children. His father, Clarence, was not an educated man. However, he had common sense and intelligence. Each time there was a job available he would read everything he could find about that particular job in the encyclopedia so that when he interviewed, he would get that job.

With the responsibility of so many children, Clarence couldn't be the Dad that Ron needed. Clarence wasn't home very much because he was working every job that he could and sometimes two jobs at a time. When he did return home, he was exhausted. With work, a wife and a pack of kids, Ron felt that he didn't get enough attention from his father.

The men of Clarence's generation were not touchy feely guys. They were tough men who fought World War II, and made sure that their families got by. Everyone in Clarence's family worked and did something to help out. When the kids weren't in school, they had jobs. They always had a roof over their heads and food on the table.

Bill Cosby once said that growing up, he didn't know he was poor, because he was loved. That was Bill Cosby's normal and that was also Ron's normal.

Clarence's health had been good until three months ago when he fell ill and was moved into a nursing home. Ron was filled with regret and sorrow for now understanding the years that he had lost and the relationship he could not retrieve with his father.

After more than an hour, with multiple cups of coffee under our belts, we were wired. The problems of the world, although not our own, had been solved. Most importantly, Ron was feeling better and he headed home. Twenty minutes later, the phone rang.

Ron had received a call from his sister. Their father was dying and Ron had to come immediately if he was going to make it in time to say good-by. He had run out of the house but his minivan wouldn't start, no matter what he did. He asked me if I could drive him to the nursing home now.

I told him to come right over.

Chicago is surrounded by over 250 individual cities creating a sprawling gridlock of streets and highways guaranteed to make any trip twice as long. Midwesterners call this vast area 'Chicagoland.' The expression, 'you can't get there from here' fits Chicagoland so perfectly that drivers don't usually think of mileage. They think in terms of how long it takes to get to their destination. A half hour drive can become an hour or two depending on the time of the day and the season.

This was going to be one of those days. In the early afternoon, we were having a winter snowstorm and even with moderate traffic, it still took us an hour and a half to get there. For both of us, it felt like forever.

The family and the nursing home administrator were waiting for Ron's arrival in the large lobby. Clarence had died while we were in route. Did Ron want to see his Dad?

Not too far into the large building was Clarence's room. The door had been closed and the lights turned off in order to not upset the other residents.

As we entered, Ron's mother switched on the overhead light bathing the room in stark utilitarian white light. This was a sad little scene. Clarence was lying in a single bed sitting low to the floor. There was room to stand, but not much more.

The administrator stayed at the door while I moved past Ron toward the window on the far side of the room allowing the family as much room as possible in the cramped quarters. As soon as I turned around, I was above everyone. There was no feeling of movement, it was simply *I was there and now I am here.*

I had the sense that time continued normally below, although I don't know how long it had, and then I was back in my body. I looked around. No one noticed what had happened. The room looked exactly like it had when we all entered. The darkness was gone. Everything was bathed in that stark overhead light and everything now had color. It was normal.

Exactly like the joke about finding a talking dog, I wasn't marveling about how amazing a talking dog is or how amazing my experience was. I was still stuck on, '*how could my body be standing there and not fall down? How does that work???*'

The afternoon had progressed and we faced a longer drive home in rush hour traffic. As distressed as he had been before, Ron would really have time to stew now.

He was quiet. He was thinking the same thoughts that anyone would. He hadn't made it in time. He didn't have a chance to tell his Dad that he loved him and he hadn't had a chance to be there when his Dad died.

Leaving the building and driving home, I wondered how to tell him that things were not at all as he thought they were. Life and death as we perceive them are not as we might imagine.

"What are you thinking?" I asked.

"I let him go. I had resolved in my own mind that - Dad you can go and I won't hold you back." He paused. "It's over for him, he seemed to be comfortable. This was the place for him to be."

I think Clarence had been an unknown third party to our conversation back at my house and that he knew Ron was on his way to the nursing home. I'm sure that he did something to Ron's van that forced him to catch a ride with me because the vehicle worked after our trip.

Above the room, Clarence had quietly let me understand that he loved his son so much more than Ron could imagine, and of course, he had waited for us to arrive. From the room to my car, I could feel the constant peaceful pressure of him pushing me to tell his beloved son 'everything.'

There lay my dilemma. If I didn't understand how this happened, how do I tell my friend? And the last thing in the world I needed was for Ron to freak out in my car.

I was in hell.

"Ah, Ron?" I sighed. "I have something to tell you."

* * *

This and many other stories appear in my book, *Spirit Knows Who You Are*, due out later this year. These are stories of hope, compassion, unfinished business, love and inspiration with people and animals who come back letting us know that they are absolutely okay and that, we on this side, are so very, very much loved.

Ann Leslie

In addition to being a former television producer/director/writer, and realtor, Ann Leslie is a published writer and a master at stained glass. When she isn't working on art commissions, writing articles and books or working in a hospice, Ann is lecturing, teaching, giving art demonstrations, running art shows, and volunteering for various governmental committees. She is also training with her local Community Emergency Response Team (CERT).

Ann is an adopted Lakota and Cherokee. She is a Pipe Keeper and advisor to various Native American groups. A student of Tibetan Buddhism, she also works with various alternative-healing modalities.

Ann currently lives with her husband and a pack of giant kissy dogs.

Ann Leslie

Spirit Knows

60-B West Terra Cotta Avenue #151

Crystal Lake, IL 60014

847-452-1925

spiritknowswho@gmail.com

Shirley Swanson

Life Lessons from Josh – A Mom and Son's Journey

"Being deeply loved by someone gives you strength, while loving someone deeply gives you courage." - <u>Lao Tzu</u>

Some life lessons slap you in the head so you will notice them, while others creep up on you softly. I've experienced both and learned to treasure them as they come. Lessons from growing up, from careers and co-workers, from friends and those who may not really rank as friends by any stretch of the imagination, from volunteering, from who-knows-where; all can shape who you are. Some of my most lasting lessons have come from family. While all three of my kids, my husband and my folks have affected me deeply, in the past few years my younger son Josh has changed my life immensely.

Josh was three years old when my husband Ted and I adopted him from an orphanage in El Salvador in 1992. He immediately bonded with our other two children Ric, 8, and Karin, 2, and we became a tight, loving family of five. While we were learning to decipher baby-talk in Spanish, Josh quickly picked up English and the rhythms of life in an American family and home. Though there were many differences, it was a terrific match and we've all been enriched.

After six months, it was discovered that Josh had Cystic Fibrosis (CF). He had nutritional and bronchial problems early in life that had seemed to be successfully dealt with at the orphanage. Those early problems now made sense in light of the diagnosis. Armed with the latest knowledge about a disease we hadn't known much about, the care of great nurses, respiratory therapists, and doctors, we moved on. Josh did well for years with a regimen of percussive therapy, pancreatic enzymes, nebulized drugs, oral and IV antibiotics and occasional hospital stays. Josh pushed himself physically, first with basketball and later with skateboarding. The exercise both strained and helped his lung capacity – one of the noticeable effects of CF. Like many youngsters, he dreamed of being a sport's pro eventually. It provided great focus and a desire to keep improving himself.

Over the years, though, the antibiotics meant to quell his CF related lung infections became less effective. His condition slowly became more complicated and critical. By the fall of 2007, his senior year in high school, his hospitalizations increased in frequency and length. He attended only 20 days of school that academic year. At the time I was teaching middle school students with severe/profound challenges in a wonderful school district one hour from home. I had never loved a job so much, but it became far harder to balance work and family needs. Caring for Josh, as well as physically and emotionally being there for the rest of the family and my students, became increasingly challenging as his health deteriorated. Home care, with the aid of home care nurses, was not easy either. Josh was "crashing" and was placed on the lung transplant list in January, 1998, after extensive tests. How do you go on when your child is coughing up copious quantities of blood from ruptured vessels in his lungs, when he's in ICU with major breathing support, when he isn't sure if he wants to live any longer because it's too hard and perhaps hopeless? I "retired" from teaching at the end of that year because Ted was finally able to get effective healthcare insurance through his college – a near miracle.

The remainder of his wait for new lungs had many incredibly rough days. I became the "go to" person for all things medical, emotional and logistical for Josh's care. Somehow, reaching out to hospital staff – nurses, social workers, respiratory therapists, doctors, plus extended family and church friends and staff, provided some balance. A few special friends were sounding boards, great listeners, and support. Though always fairly calm and steady, these were challenging times for me. I needed to listen very carefully to Josh, and work to provide balance for the family. The key was to take things step-by-step, to be positive about the potential and keep moving forward as much as possible. By knowing some of the awful possibilities that might happen, and learning what to do in advance, somehow it was easier to bear. We waited in anticipation of the possible miracle of new lungs for Josh.

Mid-morning on February 3, 2009, "the call" came. There was a potential match and Josh might finally get the new lungs/new life he so desperately needed. He had already had one "dry run" in December when it looked like there was a match, but a severe winter storm prevented the donor lungs from reaching Chicago. While he was admitted to the hospital, having blood tests, x-rays, CAT-scans and more, I notified the rest of the family. Surgery began at 6 p.m. and we were notified several hours later that all was going well. Josh was in recovery within six hours. You could hear the sigh of relief from those of us gathered in the surgical waiting room from miles away. Recovery was complicated, but Josh was home within two months. Learning the new routines, including 450 carefully timed pills a week and many self-administered tests each morning, took flexibility.

Learning to live with a future again, however, was not as easy for Josh. Physical and emotional healing did not come with an easy, upward path. Patience, listening, listening more, and care were needed by all. Support was again offered, but I knew I had to specifically seek out more. People didn't know what to offer besides food, prayer, or shopping and I learned once again to ask. It wasn't easy to admit vulnerability and ask for specific help but I learned to do it. Gift certificates to favorite family "quicker" food restaurants were welcome, as were certificates from places to pick up decent quick breakfast or lunch items. It seemed somewhat silly, but they really did make life a bit more upbeat. Help with house cleaning and organizing were invaluable. A longtime friend always organized and cleaned when she was stressed. I was just the opposite and help from friends and professional cleaners were most welcomed. Even though basically calm, stress was wearing massive holes in my memory and daily routines.

Josh's new lungs "took" and yet another new life began. He was able to finish high school, just a year late, with the aid of a wonderful tutor and great support from his school. He began community college, taking a Pharmacy Tech course since he figured he already knew so much about so many drugs! By his third year post double-lung transplant he was taking more college courses and doing so well that he was challenging himself with his true love – skateboarding. New skateboarding goals and filming others skateboarding became his passion. He was mapping out his ideal career – documenting skateboarders. In 2012 he managed to break both ankles (6 months apart) while skating. I told others, "It's wonderful that he feels so good that he can push himself hard enough to manage to break both ankles." Being patient enough to take progress as it came, and acknowledging his being well enough to skateboard with gusto and go for those ankle-breaking tricks was wonderful. His new life was moving on, and I was letting go. It was exciting to see Josh taking on his complex care while building his future.

The Spring of 2012 brought a few challenges, however. Surgeons at his medical center sought to correct a small problem. After three procedures, a slightly more invasive alternative was tried in order to prevent a more major problem in the future. Experience had taught me this procedure should take well under two hours, so when I was finally called to see the surgeon after nearly twice the time; I knew there had been a complication. What I had not expected was that it was life threatening. Taking deep breaths, listening carefully to what was being said, and trying to ask clarifying questions took all I had. The laser had flared, Josh's trachea and bronchial tubes had been burned, and the next 24 to 48 hours were critical to his chance to live. It was likely he might not make it, and if he survived there were no guarantees how he would do. This was uncharted territory. How could this have happened to my "baby"? Again, the need to take things as they came, to seek knowledge (though sparse), to gather family, and love deeply became paramount.

For five long months, Josh beat the odds and showed his strong will to live. When he was off life support and conscious, he joked that he should have let me kiss him on the forehead in pre-op earlier. It was our usual "see you later" routine when he had surgery or lesser procedures. Despite the serious condition he was in, his smiles and humor were often still there to guide the staff and family. He had more crises and miraculously made it back again from likely death. Several months into this mess, Josh required a tracheotomy to breathe. Now we needed to develop new lines of communication. This signaled the start of more serious breathing/lung issues again. At this point, he lost his ability to communicate verbally, which had been so much of a life-line between us. Enter the white-board and dry erase pens, my old friends from my days as a special education teacher. Josh alternately was frustrated by and laughed at my poor attempts to lip read what he was saying (mouthing) and to read his shaky handwriting. Amazingly, he kept his incredible smile and laugh (though now silent) for much of the nightmare.

I was at the hospital daily for those five long months. Depending on strengthened family communication, ties and love; support of hospital social work and psychology staff; friends, extended family, church, networking, volunteer and work families; helped keep us balanced. I was slightly surprised at my calmness, but it made the rest possible. Perhaps that deep love provided further courage and composure. For the past two years I had been working part time in direct sales as a certified bra fitter. This had allowed me to spend time at doctors' appointments and at the hospital, while still having some needed "me time" free of the stress. I could control my hours, still have income, and meet and support wonderful women. Others were amazed at my peacefulness and resolve, but my wonderful Josh and all my support allowed to us keep on taking this life and death ordeal as it came.

Finally, the strain was too much and Josh suffered cardiac arrest three times in one morning. He never regained consciousness, and brain damage was certain. On Sunday, October 28, 2013 we had life support removed. The family surrounded him as he took his last breaths. Josh was just 23. He was able to pass on the incredible miracle that had been given him nearly four years earlier when he received his new lungs and could breathe easily for the first time in years. At this point, Josh was able to be an organ donor despite all he had been through. As heart wrenching as it was, the family was comforted by knowing he wanted to pass on this gift. Two women now have the gift of sight and other donations were made, too. Josh, who as a youngster loved to be called "the A-M-A-Z-I-N-G Josh", was truly amazing to the end.

Many who knew Josh will always remember his warm smiles, humor, honesty, lack of pretense, and deep care for family and friends. He loved life, despite its hardships. My wish is that many will remember the gift of life – organ donation also. I will go on supporting women through my job, spreading awareness of Cystic Fibrosis, the impact on families dealing with any critical or chronic illness, and organ donation. The path may not yet be clear, but it's there and I intend to honor Josh's memory and the lessons learned. I'm looking forward to renewed commitment with enthusiasm, calm and clarity; though I know there will be tears still to come. Love will endure.

Shirley Swanson

Shirley Swanson is an artist, mom, grandma, and the "Bra Lady". She has been active with social justice and community enrichment organizations as well as being a computer graphics and fine artist, stay-at-home mom, and Special Education teacher. The valuable lessons in life that were instilled as her younger son dealt with a critical illness have made a very difficult time easier. Learning to love more deeply, listen well, empathize, seek support when needed, accept gifts and support as offered, be calm and flexible, give back, and take life one step at a time while cherishing it all are skills she treasures.

Shirley is in direct sales, holding Bra Parties and providing customized bra fittings to uplift women. Supporting women by helping them to develop great independent careers is fulfilling. This flexible career has allowed her to "be there" for her family, especially for her son Josh. It has provided a wonderful career path, support, and sanity over the rough times her family experienced recently.

Shirley is an Independent Representative for Essential Bodywear LLC and is a member of the Carol Stream Chamber of Commerce and the Lincoln Park Chapter of DPWN, the Dynamic Professional Women's Network. She lives in the Chicago area.

Shirley Swanson
Essential Bodywear LLC
630-638-3307
braladyshirley@gmail.com
www.myessentialbodywear.com/swan

Eleila Eikeland

I Want My Mamma Back
(Part One: Abridged)

BACKGROUND

A woman cradles her newborn. "What is this?" she asks the nurse.

"A pill to dry up your milk," the well-meaning nurse responds unthinkingly, according to standard practice.

"I didn't say I wanted to dry up my milk!" the mother retorts.

Decades Later

The nurse steps into the room prepared to administer medicine to an elderly woman.

"What is that?" the daughter asks from across the hospital bed.

"Antibiotics for her bladder infection," the well-meaning nurse responds unthinkingly, according to standard practice.

"It takes 24 hours for the culture. It's only been three hours since the specimen was taken." The daughter has become the advocate for the mother, who had been the advocate for the daughter decades earlier.

The nurse defends the practice. "We just want to get a jump start, in case. . ."

"We will wait." When the nurse exits, the daughter applies the appropriate aromatherapy and increases her mother's nutritional program.

THE STORY

Bounding into the kitchen through the back door, I greet my mother while she eats an apple. Though acknowledging my presence, she appears to be aloof and less alert than when I am consistently with her. So it is when I leave her to the care of others. Yet, her dementia has seen worse times. I let it go.

"Ooh. I have such pain here," she rubs her abdomen.

This is a new complaint. I suspect its condition. "Then don't eat."

One of us many siblings sits across from Mamma. I ask how the week had gone. I had just missed the departure of distant visitors who had kept Mamma busy with delightful outings during my absence. The amazing list of activities has me wonder how feats of getting her out the door in a timely manner could have been accomplished.

My attention again is drawn to Mamma's complaint. She hadn't stopped eating. Now she asks for a piece of bread. Doesn't she ever learn? Her mental challenge has become my patience challenge!

I again explain that the pain will subside by not eating, and I add, "for now". She hesitates as if to digest my words, then protests. She shall have her piece of bread!

There is no peace if she feels deprived. There is no peace if she eats and her pain worsens. So, firmly and gently, before my patience wears out, I state that she can eat later (meaning tomorrow). I then distract her by talking about my trip and the people she knows there. Her interest is perked. Then I get her ready for bed. Whew! I made it through.

Precious Moments and Belly Laughs

It isn't all wearisome. Our moments may be tender, precious and even delightful. Our topic may be about family.

"Is your mother alive?" she asks with all sincerity.

"Yes." I don't let on.

"What is she like? Is she nice?" Typical Mom, she often thinks of others and draws them into conversation.

"Oh, yes! She is superbly nice and sweet, gentle, patient, considerate, loving, forgiving, . . "

"Well, then, you take after her!" One plus of her poor memory is that she forgets that I just lost my cool ten minutes ago! "Where is your mother?" she continues. My mother is not short of questions.

"Right here!" I point to her.

(Laughter!) "Oh, how can I forget that! That is silly of me." And then she reaches out to pull me into a hug. "I'm so glad I have you as my daughter!"

We laugh through the challenges. A particular hilarious event occurred several months ago. My mother and I were sitting on the floor bursting with laughter at the silly attempts of getting her up off the floor! I creatively placed one sofa cushion on top of another in a stair arrangement. My mother was to backward crawl onto one, then the next as I wedged it under her and so on. We eventually managed but not without achy bellies from laughter.

Creating a cheerful environment works wonders for both my mother and me. Without it, discouragement slips in and eats away our energies and wills.

Hope through the Challenges

Those frequent falls back then did not bring on fractures. *Hmm. The nutritional program for bone health has been working,* I reason. Balance has also improved as she hasn't fallen for months. This increases my hope.

I see much potential in my mother. There are many days when she exhibits physical strength and mental acuity that will enable her to live years of quality life. I hold on to this hope even though it hasn't been easy to influence my mother to alter her ways. Her diminished reasoning ability dampens my trying efforts.

Family dynamics present their own challenges. If dealing with Mom isn't a large enough obstacle, my siblings frequently drop by or phone. I feel bombarded with such statements: Shouldn't Mom be eating this? She's not getting enough of that. She's lived to be over 90 on her diet, so it must work! Mom needs to take this (bottle slammed on the kitchen table). Here's the article.

She is their mother too. They are expressing concern and love (although not always conveyed in a loving manner, and *neither are my expressions*). We each want the best for Mom. We simply do not agree on what is the best.

Early on, I would add to the combat by defending my views and quoting leaders in the field. It turned out to be useless, at least for now. Evidence is in vain to those of differing persuasions.

Instead of insisting on my own way, I decide to embrace our differences and work as a team. Creating an atmosphere of appreciation would do tremendously more in the long run. Each of my siblings is supportive toward some aspects of my attempts and has praised me for them. Each has great worth to contribute to the overall benefit of our mother. I listen and consider. I make adjustments where appropriate. Therefore, I'll take the occasional squabbles to be on this terrific team!

There are countless factors impacting health. The literature is not exhausted. I welcome the articles presented to me. There is always more to learn. As I am well-aware of research bias, I read the articles sagaciously.

Return to Present Challenge: Abdominal Pain

Now, my mother's abdominal pain needs to be addressed.

A doctor confirms, "Diverticulitis," and shrugs it off as common, "especially for her age."

"Her age," I echo to myself. I reject ideas that limit well-being based upon age. I decline the prescribed pain medication, take my dear mother home, and set out my own treatment plan for her.

"Oh, I sure would like something sweet, a . . ." Mother pleas.

"No." I affirm her commitment to ridding the pain.

"Oh. *(pause)* Well, then, I do want this pain to go away," she gives in. Her discomfort is intense enough to make the right choices.

Her pain intermittently diminishes. Within three days, all of the discomfort is gone, not to return.

After six days on this program, we take a walk. She pushes her wheelchair a whole block before getting tired and sitting to ride for a while. We visit with folks along the way. She especially enjoys the cheerful toddlers who dance about her.

After three hours of sunshine and activity, we make it home. As for Mother? She is chattering delightfully of this uplifting day. She speaks of the conversations. She describes the children, their festive dress-ups and activities about her.

"Mom! You remember that?" I blurt out in surprise! She beams. "You keep this up and we can take that trip to your homeland and visit your sisters!"

She longs to go, yet has vacillated often, depending upon how she feels. If she could remember her trip and be able to get around (walker accepted), I had said I would take her.

Why Am I Here?

When I announce the good news of Mom's quick recovery from her abdominal pain and of her bonus of mental clarity, I expect my siblings to embrace her new "temporary" diet. Despite this evidence, no indication of supportive change comes.

I view obstacles as inevitable, yet temporary. This helps me to withstand times like these. Next, I ask myself why I bother with my seemingly useless attempts. Most will allow life to happen as they expect: a person ages, weakens, and dies. I see things differently.

Through my lenses, visionary possibilities open. An old person *can* live above mediocrity. Isn't it worth it to stay on to help her attain this quality of life? I am not giving up on her.

Something else keeps me posted here, at least for the time and for reasons I do not know.

I recall an incident of months ago: Mother is standing brushing her teeth while I gaze from the threshold of the bathroom contemplating stepping out for a few moments. Beyond tending to a short task, my thoughts go deeper. I've been feeling useless here. Maybe it's time to leave the caregiving to another. I make no move. Something holds me in place.

She leans on one leg and then leans more. Nevertheless, my obsession wants out. Suddenly, thoughts abruptly halt while a *Force* thrusts me forward! I dart behind her and dive into the bathtub in time to brace her fall! I block her head from impact.

I recognize this *Force* as God's power through my angel. This *Presence* held me back to where I needed to be and then thrust me forward against my resistance.

Returning to the present, it is that same *Force* that enables me to relentlessly move forward . . . *to what?* Is it to my mother's care? I accept that I do not have all the answers. But I feel assured that I have a daily *Presence* who does.

To solidify my purpose, I write out a plan. Reading it regularly helps me to persevere. I include a timeline. To devote myself indefinitely is unreasonable, and certainly not expected.

Blockade—Several Weeks Later

Mamma sits before the window. While the comical birds and squirrels at the feeder amuse her, I sit two feet away in search for airline schedules.

"We can travel in three weeks," I announce. I rise to offer her a book to read. My back turned, I reach for a . . .

"Thud!" I hear from across the room. I turn to see my dear mother on the floor! This time, she is in great pain! The X-rays at the hospital confirm a fractured hip. I sigh, *"No bright options."*

Life has unexpected twists and turns, which we often do not understand. I now take time to reflect.

I think of my desire *to have my mamma back*: the hopes of her increasing short-term memory; walking without assistance; and enjoying a visit to her homeland with me. Were these desires not to be met? Many factors outside of my devoted efforts influence the outcome. I need to accept that.

I reflect upon the many precious experiences I have had with my mother--from my earliest recollections to the recent years of reversal of roles. Then . . . (I take a deep breath), the veil over my eyes draws open to expose a precious bonding and deep love. As for getting my mamma back, I don't need to. *Mamma had always been here.*

EPILOG

We siblings hold a conference at the hospital. Viewpoints become exhausted. Heated discussions become dimmed. A decision is made. We now unify efforts for our mother's survival. Through the upcoming ordeal, we each become watchdogs and advocates for responsible medicine.

Beyond a passion, healthy longevity is my calling. Well-aware of what is at stake I relentlessly set forth my efforts to stretch beyond the survival of my mother.

The complete story is found in the book, *I Want My Mamma Back.*

Eleila Eikeland

Photo by J. Alfredo Escañuela

While being attracted to healthy lifestyles since early childhood, Eleila Eikeland soon came to believe that it is possible to become a healthy active centenarian. Her self-taught journey led her through various acclaimed yet conflictive healthy diets and treatments. She has both experienced vibrant health and ill-health as a result of her self-imposed "experiments."

Her work at and visits to numerous health resorts in North America and Europe has expanded her health horizons. Formal training and professional experiences in education, counseling and natural health has earned her recognitions as a natural health professional, educator and coach.

As a lifestyle coach, she understands the value of walking alongside her clients through the maze of healthful practices while motivating them to take action. She is a dynamic and entertaining seminar speaker who challenges her audiences to think differently. As an author, she captivates the reader by taking them on an inspiring journey. She is the author of the forthcoming book, *I Want My Mamma Back*.

For book orders or information on seminars and coaching, visit www.eikelandinst.com.

Eleila Eikeland
Eikeland Institute
rejuvenate@eikelandinst.com
www.eikelandinst.com

Alaire S. Merritt

Always Remember, to Someone...
YOU Mean the World

I was in my office on a beautiful May afternoon when I took a call that allowed me to meet someone who would change the direction of my life. A company from Utah was offering a 3-day real estate investment skills workshop. It was to be held mid-June, right as the children got out of school. The timing was perfect since they would want to be outside and our company's only scheduled work could be worked around so my husband Randy could attend with me.

As we got settled in on the first day, we met our six trainers. One of them was a retired Marine named Tony. During his 20-year Marine Corps career, he had built a company called MOTOVA8, which he introduced as one part of the program the company from Utah was offering. MOTOVA8ED is an 8 step process to "build a better you- Brains, Body and Business." The steps were:

M - Mental toughness

O - Opportunity

T - Training (physical for health)

O - Obstacles

V - Values

A - Attitude

8 steps

E - Education

D - Discipline

Each step involved practical life applications and an action plan for future use. I loved the process and was excited to find out that, if we took the real estate training with this group, there was a bootcamp that would take us through each step in depth. Randy and I decided to invest in the program so we signed up for our bootcamps as well as field training. Since we could use the skills we had developed in our sunroom business, we felt we had a head start on some of the other students and would be successful. I had a lot of hope that we would not only learn these new skills, but that I could then teach them to our children so they would not have to trade time for money and could pursue their passions in the future.

We had started our sunroom company when I was pregnant with our fourth child. After a few years, we decided to ramp up our production because we had some experience and great referrals. We did many three-day home shows to get our leads, as this was the best avenue for us to sell our products. Unfortunately, after a few years, business started to taper off as builders tore down existing residences to build monster homes. Many homeowners had decided that adding onto their house wasn't worth it because it was considered a "tear down". This inevitably led to us having fewer jobs and needing to keep funds in-house instead of paying crews unless absolutely necessary. Right about that same time, our fourth child was starting school, which freed up my days, so I started working on some of our project sites. Before our sales diminished, I had been attending two Bible studies, Moms of Preschooler meetings, and was a Girl Scout leader. Now, as I was needed to help with our business, I gradually quit these activities so that I could help Randy.

I began to feel like I was failing my precious children because I was no longer physically spending time with them. I found that we were functioning more in an "existing" atmosphere than a thriving environment. I felt like a robot, just going through the motions. My oldest daughter had left for college, which left me at home with two teenagers and one well on his way to becoming one. I was outnumbered, and emotions ran high most of the time due to the kids' age and our situation. When they were little, I had been very involved with them, every moment I possibly could be. They were my gifts from God who I had wanted all my life. Now, I felt like I had abandoned them and was not providing the nurturing environment I so desperately wanted them to experience. I wanted them to know we were a team and that we had each other's back when the world beat us up. I wanted to do a good job because I felt God had entrusted them to me so I could raise them in a way that would show Him honor and bring Him glory. And now, here I was, feeling like I was letting God down. It did not help that someone in my life often told me what a disappointment I was to them. How could I have allowed it to get to this point? This was not how I used to do things. What had changed who I was? How could I get back to God's standards? How could I reach my children's hearts so they would know their Mom and who I really was? Surely, they were not getting to see what I believed in and what my values were. I decided to start a journal at the beginning of that year so that, in case something happened to me, they could learn who I was on the inside. It would include my values, my prayers, my relationship with God and my understanding of who He was in my life, insights and quotes that I found inspiring, and my heart's desires. Most significantly, it would include the things that I felt would help them be team players in life, with others and with God. Next to those items, I wrote "TEAM", and sometimes drew smiles and hearts when something I wrote made me feel those emotions.

At the end of June, when we arrived in California for our first bootcamp (Innovate), we were happy to see one of our favorite restaurants, El Torito. We were nostalgic about El Torito because it brought back memories of all the family times we had enjoyed there back home when our children were younger, so this added to the fun and anticipation of our trip. As we walked to our hotel room, I thought, "This is the beginning of a new season in our life." The timing for this new adventure was perfect. The restaurant was within walking distance of our hotel, so we cleaned up and headed over for happy hour. We sat out on the patio in the beautiful sunshine, looking down the road lined with palm trees and munching on chips and salsa. It was awesome! In my heart, I knew we had made the right decision in attending these sessions. I was most looking forward to the next bootcamp, which was to be led by Tony and his MOTOVA8 Team.

At the end of July, when we started the MOTOVA8 bootcamp, we were given an introduction to the content of our weekend. Tony's team introduced themselves and shared a little of their personal and professional stories. Next on the agenda was to go around the room and share what we each, as participants, hoped and expected to get out of the bootcamp. I was glad that Randy and I were halfway back and that they were going through both sides of the room before hearing from our row. I needed time to really dig into my heart and find the answer. I knew what I ached for, and that was to reconnect with my children's hearts. When my turn came, I stood up to share what my heart wanted most. I had not planned to say it, but I added that I believed this team could help me to accomplish my goal. I saw something in the way Tony approached life that made me trust that his system would be well thought through and led with integrity. At the time, I knew he had served in the Marine Corps for 20 years, but I had not yet heard about how he pushed himself and endured for his team. I could not have imagined then how deeply this Marine and his stories would impact me as a mom.

As the bootcamp continued, Tony went through each of the 8 steps of MOTOVA8ED, explaining in further detail why each step was important for success, and how to apply each to our lives. This was so we could be better for those in our lives and then help others do the same. There were two steps that stood out to me as being key to moving me out of the place where I now found myself. I took each of the steps to heart because I knew if I didn't use all of the principles, it would make it impossible to change so I could achieve my desire - reconnecting with my children's hearts and being an example they could follow.

The first step I really connected with was "M" for mental toughness. The application Tony gave was: "To be successful in life, you must build a strong mind. One of the best ways to do this is to learn to deal with adversity. We are all faced with misfortune and unpleasant situations throughout life. Make the choice to learn from them! Don't let them overpower you." I recognized that this was partly what had happened to me. I had given in; feeling like I wasn't able to withstand all that was coming at me. I had become weak-minded and was allowing situations and interactions to overwhelm me. I had lost the determination to make a difference in my children's lives because I felt like there was no way to overcome all the obstacles in my way.

The next step I really connected with, and the one that gave me the most insight was "O", for obstacles. Tony explained it this way: "Obstacles give you the opportunity to enhance your mental strength. You don't have to sit back and wonder if some kind of adversity is going to come your way; in fact, you can count on it!" Our focus should be on handling and evaluating the obstacles in our lives and then taking action to deal with them. We must also believe we can do it, which goes back to mental toughness. To drive the point home, Tony had us make a list of previous obstacles and how we overcame them. Next, he asked us to write down our current obstacles and possible solutions to overcome them. If we could not come up with solutions for the obstacle, we were to ask a trusted friend to help us think of other options. The last step was to list potential future obstacles. In doing this, we could create preventative measures and try to avoid things that could become obstacles in the future. As we did this exercise, I realized that each obstacle has a solution. There are only a few options that have the possibility of resolving them so you can push through. I wrote in my notes, "JUST FACE THEM--Get it Done!!" This was eye opening, and an answer to my prayers!

As the bootcamp continued, Tony shared two stories that really hit home. The first was centered around the demonstration that airline flight attendants give before takeoff. As everyone knows, they explain that if cabin pressure is lost, an oxygen mask will drop from above your head. When you are traveling with children, you should put your mask on first and then assist them. The reasoning behind this is that, if you do not get oxygen, you will lose consciousness and be unable to support anyone else. If, however, you have access to your own oxygen source, those dependent upon you will have a chance of surviving. Somewhere along the way I had done the opposite. I had been trying to help everyone else and give them "oxygen" while I was dying from a lack of it. I thought I was helping, but I was drawing from an empty place. If I was going to make the changes I desired, I would have to find a way to get some "oxygen" so I could breathe and give of myself.

Tony's second story was about guiding his team in battle. He talked about the threats of their enemies and the planning that was needed to overcome existing or potential attacks. He showed us some photos and explained what they had to do in order to keep a step ahead and provide a way for others to pass without harm. What really hit me was Tony's statement that every decision he made could mean the difference between life and death for those who were counting on him. As I looked back at the decisions I had been making, I realized I was not making choices that would lead my team to safety, but rather was leaving them vulnerable to whatever attacks might come. It was critical for my children that I make every decision very carefully so that I could "save" my team. I also realized, for my heart to love unconditionally so I could care for my team, I would need to learn to forgive myself as well as others.

The last day of the bootcamp was hard. I was going to miss learning from and experiencing the great leadership and servanthood I saw coming from Tony and his team. They genuinely desired for us to take what we learned and to succeed in life. We were given a tool called the Life Plan that walked us through each area of our lives. It asked us to look at where we were on that day and where we wanted to be in the next 18 months. We were to complete a new Life Plan each month which would give us a snapshot of our progress in each area as well as an opportunity to set some new goals. At the end of the Life Plan was this commitment:

My name is   (Name)   and I am committed to building a better "ME"! I am willing to work hard, study hard, and follow each success step in order to maximize my growth. It is all about ME first in order to help OTHERS. Once I develop my personal and professional lifestyle, I will reach out for others to help them the way I was helped!

I am **COMMITTED and MOTOVA8ED!**

That day, I decided I was going to take what I had learned and apply it to myself first, so I could help others, starting with my children. I discovered that I can only achieve what I want in life by first changing myself. I would continue to remember Tony's enthusiasm, strength to overcome obstacles in his own life, his courage in leading his team, and his deep compassion for others. Because of his example and what I learned from him, I began my journey with God's help, to build a better me so I could lead my precious children by example, not by exception.

I share this with a grateful heart!!

I will be............ *Always Faithfully Motova8ed!!!   Alaire:-)*

Alaire S. Merritt

Alaire was born in a small town north of Jackson Tennessee and is an only child. Growing up, her mother's parents and family were very important to her and lived out two lessons she has carries with her as she walks through life. First, everyone is precious so we should treat them as we would like to be treated. Second, God allows things in our life for a purpose, gratefully accept them, and learn from them.

She has lived in Glen Ellyn for 25 years and feels blessed to be a soccer mom of 4 precious children. One of them, Danielle, married Justin in March 2013. Alaire's focus in raising her children was to create a team spirit, encourage them to follow their passions, live with a grateful attitude, always show respect to others and to have fun in life. She believes it is crucial to stay active and take care of your body since it allows you to do everything else in your life. She loves walking, biking, golfing, skiing, music and anytime she gets to dance...that's the best!!

For her, leadership starts with integrity and a servant's heart. She carried this into her role as a Girl Scout leader, as a discussion group leader for MOPS and Friday Morning Moms at her church, Glen Ellyn Bible Church and as a mom. As a leader, she understands the importance of continuing to learn from others who have been successful at developing themselves with business skills and relationships skills beyond her experience.

She and her husband, Randy, have co-owned ArborVIEW Sunrooms since 1999. ArborVIEW specializes in sunrooms, room additions, screen porches, porch conversions, decks, patios and replacement windows for the home and business. They carry an incredible 3 season window that out performs any single pane glass window for a 3 season room (not heated or cooled regularly). Their clients love this window so much that they will invest the extra expense of a full trench foundation (required by some villages) to have them in their new 3 season room. ArborVIEW featured these incredible windows in the sunrooms of several Premium Homes during the Luxury Home Tours.

Alaire has partnered with other real estate investors on two multi-family properties. She plans to use the skills she has learned as an investor, as well as the network of investors she has created, to locate and offer housing to those who have so faithfully served our country and their families.

Volunteering to serve others, especially military families, is very important to her. She feels it is an honor to serve our military heroes and their families by showing gratitude, providing comfort, resources and education through Operation Welcome You Home (WelcomeYouHome.org) and Operation Support Our Troops (OSOTAmerica.org). We can never say thank you enough!!

As this book is being assembled, she is starting a new venture called You Are Precious which gives people the opportunity to 'give from the heart'. They will provide products to communicate appreciation to others when they are given as gifts or are donated to those who deserve to be told how precious they are. The items will be a reminder to the recipient that someone believes they are precious.

Alaire S. Merritt
Glen Ellyn, Illinois
630-557-9737
ServingOurHeroes@gmail.com

You Are Precious
RememberYouArePrecious@gmail.com
www.YouArePrecious.net

ArborVIEW Sunrooms
Info@Arbor-VIEW.com
www.Arbor-VIEW.com
www.WomenContractorsConnection.com

Audrey Lowe-DeFrancesco

Graduation to Successes

me·di·oc·ri·ty the quality or state of being mediocre; of moderate or low quality, value, ability, or performance.

At age thirty five, I found myself in a mediocre place with low self esteem, ability and definitely no performance. I was in the middle of a terrible marriage that I knew I had to get out of, but how would l do this?

I felt alone having lost my mother to cancer ten years earlier and my father who had taken an overseas position. My two main mentors and supporters were gone.

I knew I couldn't stay in the abusive marriage for myself but more importantly for my two daughters who were then twelve and ten. I did not want them to think that the way I being treated was okay for not only me but also for them. This "marriage" was not a partnership. There was no respect, love, companionship, trust or anything of value.

I honestly dreaded to do the scariest thing ever in my life and that was to file for divorce. I felt as if I could climb up the wall and I convinced myself "you can do it". However, hurdling over it was very difficult since it was not only a hurdle for myself but for them as well.

There were major decisions such as: Where do I live? What do I do? How do you start over after thirteen years of being a repressed housewife?

Going into life as a single mother my goal was to set an example and to raise my daughters to be strong independent women. I wanted them to be happy with who they had become.

So I found a job doing what I loved the most, which was writing and photographing for a local newspaper. It was a job that was close to home and close to my daughters. I worked on features, human interest stories, the school beat and a photo opinion column. Since I was formally trained as a film photographer, working at the newspaper taught me about the new emerging world of digital photography. I also found a home in the same school district so that the girls could remain in the same schools and have the same friends. Since their home and their father was gone, this kept a constant in their very changing lives.

The years after the divorce were better but not easy. Having to put my daughters through college took me away from my job at the newspaper into an insurance career for which I was formally trained and licensed to sell.

Over the next ten years, it wasn't always easy to keep them on the track to succeed and to be strong and independent. Having to be a mom and dad meant I had to intervene with friends who could have influenced them to travel down the wrong paths, boyfriends who interfered with decision making and life choices. Let's just say I was not always the popular parent.

As they grew older, I let them learn by their own mistakes. I watched them make them and guided them through them. Since we all make mistakes, it's how they are handled and explained so they can be avoided that is most important.

Thirteen years later, I can say that my greatest accomplishment was the day I saw them both walk across the stage to receive their college diplomas.

As I sat in the auditorium, I could reflect back to the times in my mind when they graduated from kindergarten, middle school, and high school. To see these wonderful young women -confident, strong, knowledgeable and worldly accept their degrees, it was more than a diploma. It was an accomplishment that I promised to myself that they would be the strong independent and successful young women that they both had become.

Now working in a field like insurance and photography that I love, being in a relationship where I am loved, and knowing my daughters will reach the sun moon and stars have resulted in overcoming mediocrity. I have set an example and guiding them into a better place. My wish is that we never have to experience mediocrity.

When we raise our children it's natural that when they are infants to want to hold every part of them securely in our fists controlling everything that they do, where they go, what they eat and who they are with. Gradually, as they age, we open our fists very slowly until they are standing up right balancing on the palm. However, we remain the platform and the reassurance in their lives. When they decide to jump off, nothing is more exciting than to sit back and watch them enter into their own lives, see them succeed and know that you have also succeeded to overcome mediocrity.

I want to thank my brother, sister in law, father and friends. You know who you are, for your support through it all. I want to thank everyone who helped encourage me without whom I would not be the person I am today.

Audrey Lowe-DeFrancesco

I took my first photography class in 1976 while in the 7th grade. It laid the foundation for my love of capturing photos and the evolution of what I see through a lens today. I was surprisingly recognized for my 1998 photos of the newly erected *Petronis Towers in Kuala Lumpar Malaysia and *Mui Wo, a Buddhist sanctuary in Hong Kong, China. Four of the photos were published in the National Library of Congress in 1999. "It's wonderful when your work gets recognized and published. However other pieces do not. Nevertheless, all of my photography is very personal and sentimental to me."

My work as a photojournalist 2000 to 2003 for *Examiner Publications in the Tri Village area opened up a comfort zone to "getting the shot" and doing whatever it takes to get it. It definitely added confidence and fine tuning to my work. I primarily covered writing and photographing for news sections that included features and human interest, school beat, entertainment, and historical columns including a weekly photo opinion column. I also photographed special events, local government, board and village meetings and anything that was community and locally related. My travels have inspired my work by exposing me to new material in many areas of the world. Although these places were already captured on film they gave me the challenge of creating a new twist to the art of storytelling through photography. In 2010, I was accepted into the Elmhurst Art Guild and am preparing to exhibit my art in the spring art show. I have been fortunate to have been reimbursed for my photographs by: designers, musicians, dancers, actors, families, expectant moms, graduates, fashion shows, private gardens, athletes, and to catalog artists collections.

Audrey Lowe-DeFrancesco
Audrey Lowe Photography
286 Windsor Drive
Bartlett, IL 60103
630-830-0437
Adancerz2@aol.com
http://adancerz2.wix.com/audreylowephoto

Deborah Battersby

Waking Up Happy

Do you wake up happy?

I want to wake up happy. I want to be excited and energized about life and all its majesty. I want to believe in me, in you and our Higher Purpose here on this planet. I want to be stoked about how we can use our unique gifts and combine our talents to make this world better just because we showed up here, now.

If this isn't one of your goals, then don't read this chapter, because it's about getting back to being genuinely happy, and for some of us that may mean getting there for the first time. If being happy is something you'd given up on then keep reading. There's some insight here for you that will restore your faith and give you certainty that happiness is definitely something you can not only have but you're absolutely, positively supposed to have. And if being happy is something you crave, you're going to love knowing how to get to it and live in it consistently.

Most of my clients are high achieving entrepreneurs and even the most successful among them say they want to be happy or happier. Though they've had stellar accomplishments in business and career, a common lament is "there's still something's missing." These hard-working folks have everything they thought they would ever need to be happy but they aren't. Why not? Shouldn't they, shouldn't we all get to be happy?

Until recently the idea of happiness didn't come anywhere near my goals, vision board or bucket list. It was always about success and achievement. I didn't strive to be happy. There was always this back of my mind assumption that if I got this or that "thing" handled then happiness would just show up. If I got down to the right jeans size, made more money, got my kids through college or made better investments then I could be, would be happy. I spent many decades on that treadmill putting one goal after another in front of me assuming the next one would finally be the one that would deliver not only happiness, but happily ever after.

Don't get me wrong; I had bouts of happiness or at least satisfaction after the achievement of certain goals and milestones but it just didn't last. Sometimes it was so fleeting it brushed by like a breeze, invisible to the eye and impossible to grasp.

What started this conversation we're having is this. One morning I woke up with a strange question. "Am I happy?" It was weird that it would be my first conscious thought of the day. The usual ones are more like: "What do I have to do today?; Where do I have to be?; Who did I promise what?; What time is my first appointment?"

Is that how it goes for you too? In any case, "Am I happy?" was not a typical day-starting thought. I have, from time to time, noticed the kind of mood I woke up in: happy, excited, optimistic, angry, worried, cranky, etc. There are also those times when others were quick to point out what "side" of the bed I woke up on, especially when it was the "wrong side".

But the bigger question is: Are you supposed to wake up happy? Is that even an option? Was there a time, any time, even as a kid when you felt truly happy and woke up energized and excited about the day? If you did, do you still? If you don't, did it suddenly stop one day, without notice, or was it more of a gradual dwindling away? Was it a matter of getting out of the habit of being happy or more like getting into the habit of being stressed, distracted, disinterested or judgmental?

I wondered, is being happy something that happens to you or is it something you do, or could it be something you stop doing? Maybe it's all of the above. Let's see what happens if we consider or even combine all three.

1. **Something you do:** One of the easiest things you can do to turn your mood around is to smile. Do you know people who just seem to smile all the time? It's contagious isn't it? Even if you're grumpy when you see them, sooner or later their smiles have a way of shaking things up and lifting your spirits. You can't help but feel good around them.

   Smiling is not something most people are in the habit of doing—I know I wasn't.

   On a particularly stressful afternoon, I needed to clear my head and decided that a change of scenery would do me good. So, I ventured out into the fresh air for a walk in the forest preserve behind my house. To lighten things up and shake off the pressure I felt, I set an intention to smile the entire walk, all three miles. It was easier said than done. I was surprised how much concentration it required. Smiling was obviously not a regular habit for me. The instant I let my attention wander, I wasn't smiling anymore and had to remind myself to get back to smiling. By the end of my walk, it dawned on me that all these years I had been waiting for things to make me happy and to make me smile. It was like it was the job of the outside world to ensure my happiness instead of realizing I could decide to be happy. I could choose to smile and make myself happy first.

   I had the best and most energizing experience because while I was smiling. I could not fret over anything. Seriously: try it. I've had plenty of walks where I focused on deadlines, responsibilities and putting out fires. There was definitely no smile on my face and while it was still beneficial just to take the break and get some exercise, something magical happened when I added the smile. My experience was radically different. The route was the same, but the scenery was far more vibrant. My pace was peppier, and my thoughts wandered toward playful, creative optimism. I returned to my desk refreshed, uplifted, happy and ready to work.

Try starting your day with 15 minutes of smiling. Uninterrupted, no matter what or where, just smile.

Take a minute to jot down the changes in your mood and attitude toward your day.

_____

_____

_____

_____

_____

Top 10 Reasons to Wear Your Smile:

1. **Making yourself smile can boost your mood:** Psychologists found that even if you're in bad mood, you can instantly lift your spirits by smiling.

2. **Smiling boosts your immune system:** Your body is more relaxed when you smile, which contributes to good health and a stronger immune system.

3. **Smiles are contagious:** It's not just a saying: smiling really is contagious.

4. **Smiling Relieves Stress**: Your body immediately releases endorphins when you smile, even when you force it.

5. **It is easier to smile than to frown:** Scientists have discovered that your body has to work harder and use more muscles to frown than it does to smile.

6. **Smiling is a universal sign of happiness:** While hand shakes, hugs, and bows all have varying meanings across cultures, smiling is known around the world and in all cultures as a sign of happiness and acceptance.

7. **Smile at work:** Smiling at work actually makes you more productive and helps you enjoy your work more.

8. **Smiles use from 5 to 53 facial muscles**: Just smiling burns calories and can require your body to use up to 53 muscles.

9. **Smiling helps you get promoted:** Smiles make a person seem more attractive, sociable and confident, and therefore more likely to get promoted.

10. **Smiles are more attractive than makeup:** A research study conducted by Orbit Complete discovered that 69% of people find women more attractive when they're smiling.

****

2. **Something you stop doing:** Your happiness quotient can be substantially elevated when you stop doing certain things. This is one of my favorites from Dr. Wayne Dyer: Stop Complaining.

Achieving results you want sometimes means you have to stop putting up your own roadblocks. Take complaining, for example, this one can sneak up on you because it seems so innocent in the beginning, more like you're merely stating facts. Listen in:

"I'm exhausted I didn't get much sleep last night. This cold and sinus headache just wouldn't let me rest. Then I overslept. The kids were cranky. Traffic was a bear. Drivers are so rude. I got cut off and missed my exit. My boss glared at me when I came in just 3 minutes late, etc, etc, etc." Sound familiar?

The trouble with complaining is:
- Each upset gets stacked on top of another.
- It hijacks your focus and goes to what isn't working or fair.
- People join in to commiserate and things escalate.
- It's highly contagious and spreads quickly.
- Energy dips as self-induced frustration mounts.
- Life looks and feels increasingly unfair.
- It primes you to find even more to complain about.

Take this 24-hour challenge, if you're up for it . . .

- Declare a No-Complaining Day! This means NO complaining for 24 hours. If you find yourself complaining silently, just say STOP! If or when it happens again, repeat: STOP. It'll be useful to notice how often the practice of complaining shows up. You'll be excited by how much more in control you feel when complaining is no longer a conditioned response to challenges.

- At the end of the 24 hours, grab this book and jot down a few words about your day and what you learned from it.

_____

_____

_____

_____

You get to take charge of your happiness by stopping a few little things that get in the way of your best results.

****

3. **Something that happens:** Stuff happens in everyone's life, some of it great, some good, some bad, some beyond horrible. How we look at it, feel about it and deal with is a choice that can become habit.

You know "the glass is half empty", "the glass is half full" and "the glass is full" viewpoints refer to the same glass with the same amount of liquid. What's different is how the glass is perceived and described. The half empty glass is focused on what is missing; the half full glass notices what's there, while the full glass describes a container half full of liquid and half full of air. Choosing either perspective is easy because they're all true. However, the way you look at it and the language you use to describe the glass and its contents sets up the mindset for how you see everything.

I'm not suggesting that your choice changes anything that has happened to you, but I am suggesting that it can change how you respond to what happens and what subsequent actions you will or won't take. Creating and maintaining the "half full" or "full" mindset can be done with questions. The questions you ask yourself direct your focus and tell you what to pay attention to. What you tell your mind/unconscious to look for it will find.

Here are a few questions to try out:

What is great or good about this?

How does this serve me &/or the people I care about?

What can I learn from this?

How can I use this to help others and myself?

What can I be grateful for in this situation?

My passion is helping committed entrepreneurs happily achieve everything they want… without working harder and while having lots more fun. It's good for the environment and all of us because as human beings we are kinder, more industrious, more creative and more loving when we are happy. It is my sincere hope that these simple reminders will seep into your heart and mind so that you can have lots more happiness in your life and sprinkle some of it into the lives of others. The world could sure use it!

Deborah Battersby

Deborah Battersby, known as the Success Accelerator, is a business & performance coach. Using NLP and pattern recognition to solve the "individual success puzzle", Deb helps her clients put the right elements together for faster, easier results.

Award-winning achievement is not new to Deb or her clients and why some, like Dr. Sam Hazledine, of MedRecruit, Ernst & Young 2012 Young Entrepreneur of the Year, call her his "secret weapon."

An avid puzzle geek and mystery buff, Deb is intrigued with problem-solving and clue gathering. "What makes some people succeed while others fail?" presented a puzzle that initiated a 12 year quest resulting in the emMatrix Coaching Model ™ which allows Battersby to take behavioral transformation and human potential to new heights

As an RRI master trainer Tony Robbins has trusted his VIPs and personal guests to Deb for 15 years. Her coaching methods have helped thousands create fast, effective changes to accelerate success without working any harder.

Deborah Battersby
Success Matrix
PO Box 8111
Bartlett, IL 60103
630-830-0064
deb@SuccessMatrix.com
www.deborahbattersby.com

OVERCOMING
Mediocrity©
Volume II

Coming in the Fall of 2013

www.overcomingmediocrityteam.com